POCKET

CHARLESTON & SAVANNAH

TOP SIGHTS · LOCAL EXPERIENCES

D0950447

ASHLEY HARRELL, MASOVAIDA MORGAN

Contents

Plan Your Trip

Welcome to Charleston
& Savannah..........................4

Top Sights...........................6

Eating.................................10

Drinking & Nightlife.........12

Shopping...........................14

History...............................16

Hauntings.........................18

Romance...........................19

The Outdoors...................20

The Arts.............................21

Four Perfect Days...........22

Need to Know..................24

Charleston
Neighborhoods...............26

Savannah
Neighborhoods...............27

Cathedral of St John the Baptist (p115),
Savannah MEUNIERD/SHUTTERSTOCK ©

Explore Charleston

South of Broad & the French Quarter.................31

East Side, NoMo & Hampton Park...................45

Harleston Village, Upper King & Cannonborough Elliotborough.......................61

Charleston County Sea Islands..........................77

Beaufort & Hilton Head Island...........95

Explore Savannah

Historic District & Forsyth Park.....................107

Midtown & the Victorian District.............123

East Savannah & the Islands.........................135

Worth a Trip

Fort Sumter National Monument.........90

Wormsloe Historic Site.....................144

Survival Guide 147

Before You Go.................148

Arriving in Charleston & Savannah......................149

Getting Around..............150

Essential Information.....151

Special Features

Old Slave Mart Museum..............................32

Aiken-Rhett House...........46

McLeod Plantation............78

Forsyth Park....................108

Laurel Grove Cemetery.........................124

Bonaventure Cemetery..........................136

Welcome to Charleston & Savannah

The zenith of old-world charm, Charleston whisks you into the nation's tumultuous past and nourishes your mind, heart and stomach in roughly equal measure. Still hungry? Just two hours south, Savannah is rife with elegant town houses, antebellum mansions, green public squares, pristine tidal freshwater marshes and mammoth oak trees bedecked in moss.

Top Sights

MEUNIERD/SHUTTERSTOCK ©

Fort Sumter National Monument

Charleston's most noteworthy historic fort. **p90**

DARRYL BROOKS/SHUTTERSTOCK ©

Forsyth Park

A lively, outdoor delight in Savannah. **p108**

McLeod Plantation

A true education on slavery at a Charleston County Sea Islands plantation. **p78**

Bonaventure Cemetery

Savannah's hauntingly stunning Southern Gothic necropolis. **p136**

Old Slave Mart Museum

Charleston's most important history museum. **p32**

Wormsloe Historic Site

Savannah's enchanting estate. **p144**

Laurel Grove Cemetery

Savannah's most historic resting place. **p124**

Aiken-Rhett House

Charleston's most interestingly preserved home. **p46**

Eating

Kiss your grits – you're in fine eatin' country. Lowcountry cuisine dominates the scene in both Charleston and Savannah, drawing from land (okra, field peas, rice and corn) and sea (shellfish), and heavily influenced by West/Central African traditions brought via the slave trade.

Dining Out in Charleston

Its chefs are regular contenders for James Beard awards. Its restaurants and dishes frequently get the nod from magazines like *Bon Appétit*. And with culinary roots in Europe, the Caribbean and West Africa, is it any wonder that every year millions of people pack a toothbrush just to eat in Charleston? But reading or hearing about delicious things never quite satisfies

the way, say, slurping a raw oyster can. Or tearing into a fried green tomato. Or swirling the cream and sherry in a bowl of she-crab soup...

Dining Out in Savannah

Savannah is known as the 'Hostess City of the South' – and a good hostess will stuff you to the gills with all things battered and fried before sending you on your merry way. This is a city where people

come to indulge in decadent, traditional Southern and soul food, but top chefs are also reimagining things with a 'New South' cuisine, where classic themes and ingredients meet innovative preparations. With Savannah's proximity to the ocean, seafood features heavily on most menus, and good grub doesn't stop at Southern staples – fans of diverse international fare can find great options, too.

BONCHAN/SHUTTERSTOCK ©

Best Restaurants

Tu A playful Charleston restaurant with creative and mind-blowing international dishes. (p54)

Husk Savannah Scaled-up Southern dishes made with ingredients from local purveyors. (p116)

167 Raw Hole-in-the-wall that unassumingly serves up Charleston's best seafood. (p53)

FIG Long-time Charleston foodie haven with great service and top-notch nouvelle Southern fare. (p54)

Mrs Wilkes Dining Room Rich, traditional, communal-style Southern fare in Savannah. (p116)

Best Dishes

Shrimp and Grits (pictured) Arguably the Lowcountry's most famous dish, enjoyed in varying preparations at restaurants all over town.

Lowcountry Boil Shell-on shrimp, corn on the cob, sausage and red potatoes boiled or steamed together with spices. Spread sheets of newspaper on a table, dump out the pot and get to grubbin'.

Fried Green Tomatoes Unripened tomatoes get sliced and coated with a cornmeal batter before taking a plunge into sizzling bacon fat or lard. Top 'em with pimento cheese and bacon for an extra-sinful experience, or crown a salad with a slice or two and feign being healthy.

She-Crab Soup Named for the crab roe garnish (which many restaurants leave off), this rich, creamy soup usually includes lumps of blue-crab meat, sherry and plenty of spice.

Barbecue From the Carolinas to Texas, low and slow pit-smoked protein is a US claim to fame, and Savannah and Charleston both excel at it.

Buttermilk Biscuits Whether you get 'em smothered in gravy or piled with pimento cheese, this quintessential Southern snack will have your taste buds singing.

Drinking & Nightlife

The denizens of these fine cities have a famous appreciation of all things nightlife. Balmy Charleston evenings are perfect for a cool cocktail or dancing to live jazz, while Savannah's revelers often take advantage of the lax open-container regulations, bouncing from downtown watering holes to hidden haunts and bars along rollicking nightlife corridors.

Charleston by Night

Charleston may be a genteel city, but its residents are not above throwing a few back and having a good ole time. There's always something shakin' here, be it a boozy RiverDogs ball game, a highly anticipated concert at a local music venue, or swing-dance lessons at a hoppin' speakeasy. The craft-beer scene has taken off, with the best concentration of breweries in the Northern Penin-sula, Mt Pleasant and North Charleston, and a brews cruise to help you hit four breweries in one. Craft distilleries are also on the rise, with two good ones right downtown.

Partying in Savannah

Savannah (pictured) knows how to have a good time – and we're not just talking the throngs of green-clad party-goers who descend upon the city for St Patrick's Day (Savannah's celebra-tion is second only to New York City for the largest in the world). Though a modestly sized city, the nightlife turns up year-round. The watering holes are aplenty, from the tourist-frequented hubs along River St, south to the bumpin' dance clubs on Congress St, and to the locals' dives in the Victorian District. The best part? You can take boozy drinks 'to go' in plastic cups and saunter through downtown without dropping that buzz.

SEAN PAVONE/SHUTTERSTOCK ©

Best for Craft Booze in Charleston

Edmund's Oast A fancy brewpub with 64 taps and fine food like salt chicken skins, hanger steaks and hot-and-sour tilefish. (p54)

Firefly Distillery The home of America's first sweet-tea vodka, and also lots of other outrageously delicious and intoxicating liquors. (p88)

High Wire Distilling In downtown Charleston, get your tastes of small-batch gin, whiskey, vodka and amaro, right in a row. (p71)

Prohibition A speakeasy-style craft cocktail bar where you can take swing-dancing lessons. (p72)

Best for Live Music in Savannah

Savannah Smiles Dueling Pianos Croon crowd-selected favorites off rowdy River St. (p121)

El-Rocko Lounge Hip cocktail bar that regularly hosts indie, rock, soul and funk bands. (p118)

Jinx Metal, rock, alt-country and hip-hop acts blast the stacks in this gloriously grungy, small-scale venue. (p121)

House of Strut Vintage store by day and performance venue by night, where local bands jam for the hometown crowd. (p131)

Boozy Bus

Charleston Brews Cruise (☏843-860-7847; https://charlestonbrewscruise.com; 375 Meeting St; drinker/nondrinker $65/25; ⊙tours 1:30pm Sun & Tue-Thu, 12:30pm Fri & Sat) runs buses around to a rotating selection of four local breweries.

Shopping

Whether it's Lowcountry gifts, fine art and antiques, vintage garments or local farmers market products you seek, these two shopping hubs have got you covered.

Charleston

The Historic District is clogged with over-priced souvenir shops and junk markets. Head instead to King St: hit lower King for antiques, middle King for cool boutiques and upper King for trendy design and gift shops. Or try the main stretch of Broad St, dubbed 'Gallery Row.'

Savannah

West Broughton St is Savannah's pre-eminent shopping district – with both corporate and indie entities shoulder to

shoulder, and all of it punctuated with a distinctly SCAD (Savannah College of Art and Design) flavor. There are also great options close to the riverfront and further south in the Victorian District.

Best Shopping in Charleston

Charleston City Market You can wander the stalls here for hours checking out local crafts and food products, such as hand-made sweetgrass. (p43; pictured)

Farmers Market Everybody comes here for local pro-duce, homemade food and

drinks, art, music, boiled peanuts and more. (p75)

Charleston Crafts Cooperative Contemporary South Carolina–made crafts, including sweetgrass baskets, hand-dyed silks and wood carvings. (p75)

Best Shopping in Savannah

ShopSCAD Pick up something unique and handmade by a local art-school student, faculty member or alum. (p121)

Books on Bay Quaint shop selling sweet vintage and antique books. (p119)

House of Strut Purveyor of thoughtfully curated vintage fashion, with local creative events in the same space. (p131)

JAMES KIRKIKIS/SHUTTERSTOCK ©

Best Food & Beverage Stores in Savannah & Charleston

Savannah Bee Company
Taste a variety of artisanal honeys at this renowned purveyor. (p121)

Tavern at Rainbow Row
America's oldest liquor store, with free weekend whiskey tastings. (p43)

Charleston Tea Plantation
There's a great gift shop here, with sets of tea bags from the only tea plantation in the US. (p84)

Goat. Sheep. Cow. North.
A gourmet cheese shop in Charleston's NoMo that triples as a cafe and wine bar. (p59)

Best Places to Shop for Art

ShopSCAD Fine art, jewelry, gifts and apparel made by Savannah College of Art and Design students and alums. (p121)

Robert Lange Studios
Charleston's most renowned contemporary art gallery. (p43)

Two Women & A Warehouse
Creatively repurposed furniture pieces and art from local vendors in Savannah. (p133)

W Hampton Brand Gallery
A gallery in Charleston's South of Broad neighborhood selling slate roof tiles with Rainbow Row painted on them in. (p43)

Worth a Trip: Bluffton

Just a quick jaunt over the Harbor River and you're in Bluffton – Hilton Head's quaint sister city, which is brimming with art studios, antebellum homes and Lowcountry charm. Artsy types will appreciate Calhoun St, which is lined with quirky galleries and shops.

History

In Charleston and Savannah, concerted efforts are made to keep the past in the present. In other words, everywhere you look there is a home, or a fort or even an entire neighborhood that calls a previous century to mind.

Charleston

This lovely city will embrace you with the warmth and hospitality of an old and dear friend – who lived in the 18th century. We jest, but the cannons, cemeteries and carriage rides absolutely conjure an earlier era. Here, signers of the Declaration of Independence puffed cigars and whispered of revolution in the withdrawing rooms of historic homes, and the first shots of the Civil War rang out over Fort Sumter in Charleston Harbor. The city itself was built on slave labor, and several related sights are among the nation's most important educators on the long-standing oppression of African Americans.

Savannah

As the first city and original capital of Georgia – the last of the 13 British colonies before the United States were formed in 1776 – Savannah's history is robust and replete with accounts to keep any buff wandering its streets, squares and haunts in pursuit of storied tales. There are historic buildings and monuments around every turn, and tours for all tastes, shedding light on topics like the establishment of the city, Savannah's role in the transatlantic slave trade, the siege that became the second deadliest battle of the Revolutionary War – and that's just the beginning.

JASON TENCH/SHUTTERSTOCK ©

Best Historical Sights in Charleston

Aiken-Rhett House 'Preserved as found,' this 1820 town house showcases the lifestyle of a wealthy merchant's family and the people they enslaved. (p46)

McLeod Plantation An old Sea Island cotton plantation whose story encapsulates a larger one about slavery and emancipation in the South. (p78)

Fort Sumter National Monument See where the Civil War began, and take selfies with some old cannons. (p90)

Old Slave Mart Museum This small museum offers an important (and highly disturbing) explanation of how Charleston's prominence and wealth came from slave labor. (p32)

Middleton Place This plantation's vast gardens are the oldest in the US. (p57)

Charleston Museum The country's first museum is well organized, digestible and full of interesting artifacts and information. (p52)

Best Historical Sights in Savannah

Wormsloe Historic Site Famous for the stunning entrance to the grounds, which features a canopy of 400 live oak trees. (p144)

Fort Pulaski National monument with guided tours, a museum and trails that are great for walking and biking. (p141; pictured)

American Prohibition Museum Immersive exhibitions and storytelling shed light on prohibition in this one-of-a-kind museum. (p115)

Hauntings

AIMEE M LEE/SHUTTERSTOCK ©

Charleston and Savannah are considered by many to be two of the most haunted cities in America, and for good reason. The tumultuous histories of these cities are inextricably tied to the slave trade and the Confederacy, and countless battles were fought in and around them.

Haint Blue

While visiting Charleston and Savannah, you'll notice lots of porch ceilings painted 'haint' blue (pictured above). This color was thought by the Gullah people to ward off evil 'haints' (spirits), and is also said to deter insects as well.

Spook Read

The book *Midnight in the Garden of Good and Evil* offers a good introduction to Savannah's eerie side.

Best Ways to Get Spooked in Charleston

Old South Carriage Co Offers a haunted carriage ride after dark. (p54)

Bulldog Tours Has a spooky night tour that stops at the Old City Jail, Provost Dungeon and the city's oldest graveyard. (p40)

Dock Street Theatre There have been regular sightings of ghosts in the rafters here, though some believe they're failed actors. (p42)

Poogan's Porch *Ghost Dog* is more than a Jim Jarmusch film; this place is said to be haunted by the dog it's named after. (p68)

Best Ghost Experiences in Savannah

Bonaventure Cemetery Savannah's most famous city of the dead is at once harrowing and enchanting. (p136)

Laurel Grove Cemetery Split into two parts – one for whites and one for blacks – both are worth visiting for their historical significance. (p124)

Sorrel Weed House A seriously spooky mansion with grand architecture and hair-raising tours. (p114)

Romance

BONNIE DAVIDSON/SHUTTERSTOCK ©

These charming, intimate cities are the sorts where visitors tend to revel in the simple beauty of walking around. Whether you're solo or coupled up, you'll fall in love with the well-preserved history and the twisting oak trees that line the quaint avenues of these two fair cities.

Charleston is for Lovers

Charleston's most beloved 19th-century porch furnishing was the joggling board – a bouncy, wooden rocking bench that couples sat on as part of a courtship ritual. Not much has changed. Today lovers stroll cobblestone streets past historic buildings, stop to smell the blooming jasmine and enjoy long, candlelit dinners on verandas. Everywhere you turn, another blushing bride is standing on the steps of yet another enchanting church. Charleston will charm the sweat right off your brow.

Falling for Savannah

People are drawn to Savannah for its enchanting scenery, its leisurely pace of life and the endearing, soulful Savannahians who embolden everyone to let their freak flags fly. Have a wander through the Historic District and you're bound to strike up a conversation with alluring passersby, or sit for a time with someone special on the benches around the iconic fountain in Forsyth Park.

Best Romantic Experiences

Forsyth Park Home to Savannah's iconic fountain, which sits smack in the middle of a sprawling green space. (p108)

Middleton Place The vast gardens of this plantation outside Charleston are the oldest in the US. (p57; pictured)

Olde Pink House The atmosphere of this 18th-century mansion in Savannah is worth a visit alone; the food is just as good. (p117)

Zero Café + Bar Small, intimate Charleston establishment with a killer tasting menu. (p56)

The Outdoors

With bridges to islands at seemingly every turn, Charleston and Savannah are prime destinations for beachgoers, boaters and basically anyone who likes to look out over the water. Each city also offers some wonderful day trips to nearby wetlands, lowland forests and nature parks.

VINCE DOYLE/SHUTTERSTOCK ©

Getting on the Water

Without a boat friend in Savannah or Charleston, you'll need to call upon one of the local tour operators. In Savannah, a top choice is **Wilderness Southeast** (☏912-236-8115; www.wilderness-southeast.org; prices vary by tour & number of people), which offers wilderness adventures by motorboat and kayak. In Charleston, ring up **Nature Adventures Outfitters** (☏843-568-3222; www.kayakcharlestonsc.com; Shrimp Boat Lane; tours adult/child from $45/35; ☉8am-

8pm May-Sep, hours vary rest of year). They lead local saltwater and blackwater kayak and canoe trips, as well as overnight trips down farther-flung rivers. **Adventure Harbor Tours** (☏843-442-9455; www.adventureharbortours.com; 56 Ashley Point Dr; adult/child 3-12yr $55/30) is a recommended

operator for shelling trips to Morris Island.

Best Outdoor Destinations

Little Tybee Island This off-the-grid natural wonder is a draw for true adventure seekers. (p140)

Bulls Island (pictured above) Offers hiking trails, shelling, alligators and a 'boneyard' beach with spooky, bare trees poking up through the sand. (p86)

Top Tips

○ Pack a bathing suit, particularly if you're visiting in the spring, summer or fall.

○ Prepare to do a lot of walking; it's the best way to experience these cities.

The Arts

Dubbed the Creative Coast, Savannah boasts a vibrant arts and design scene that's fueled by the Savannah College of Art and Design (SCAD). Meanwhile, Charleston boasts a couple of fantastic galleries and art museums, and offers a delightful art walk on the third Thursday of each month.

DIFFERENT_BRIAN/GETTY IMAGES ©

Savannah's Art Scene

SCAD is one of the finest art schools in the country, with students and faculty from far and wide. The city's art scene is also bolstered by the natives and transplants whose initiatives make the arts more inclusive and accessible. From superb museums and galleries in the Historic District to locally crafted pursuits in the Starland section, creativity is the lifeblood coursing through Savannah's artsy heart.

Charleston's Art Scene

The city's artsiest stretch, Broad St, is known as 'Gallery Row.' More than 40 galleries here and around the rest of the city participate in Art-Walk (p43). Another of the city's artistic achievements is the Charleston Step, a dramatic dance often set to ragtime jazz. It is the basis of modern swing dancing, and is thought to have been invented by African Americans living on islands near the city in the early 1900s.

Best Places to Appreciate Art

SCAD Museum of Art Contemporary art and design museum with 4500 works in its impressive permanent collection. (p114)

Redux Contemporary Art Center Charleston's contemporary art hub and event space, with three galleries and a few dozen studios. (p52)

Gibbes Museum of Art A contemporary collection in Charleston including works by local artists, with Lowcountry life as a highlight. (p66)

Telfair Academy In Savannah, the oldest public art museum in the South houses 19th- and 20th-century American and European works. (p114; pictured above)

Four Perfect Days

Day 1, Charleston

Spend a couple of hours meandering around Charleston's awe-inspiring **Historic District** (p31), or jump on a tour with **Charleston Footprints** (p40).

Take lunch at **Gaulart & Maliclet** (p40) or **Poogan's Porch** (p68), then visit the **Old Slave Mart Museum** (p32). Continue on for a tour of the **Nathaniel Russell House** (p38), or time-travel to the 1700s with a tour of the **Heyward-Washington House** (p38; pictured above).

Feast at **FIG** (p54) or drop into **167 Raw** (p53), then stroll the city, popping in and out of any cocktail bar that catches your eye. For a great view of the city at night, head for **Pavilion Bar** (p42) or **Rooftop at the Vendue** (p42).

Day 2, Charleston

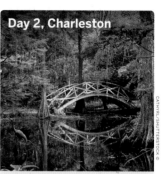

Hit the Ashley River plantations. **Drayton Hall** (p57) features the oldest plantation house in America. **Magnolia Plantation** (p57; pictured above) offers a magnificent swamp tour. **Middleton Place** (p57) has the oldest gardens in the US, and they are exquisite.

Return to the city for lunch at Bill Murray's **Harold's Cabin** (p55). Do a lazy afternoon of craft boozing at places like **Revelry Brewery** (p56).

For dinner, stop in at **Edmund's Oast** (p54) for fine gastropub fare, or venture into **Workshop** (p58) for experimental dishes from top chefs. Attend a minor league ball game at **The Joe** (p59) or try a spooky ghost walk with **Bulldog Tours** (p40).

Day 3, Savannah

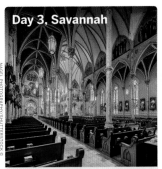

Soak in the Southern charm in Savannah's Historic District. Start at the south end of **Forsyth Park** (p108) and be sure to see the fountain and Marine Memorial. Amble up Bull St to Monterey Sq and **Mercer-Williams House** (p114).

Take a decadent Southern lunch at **Mrs Wilkes Dining Room** (p116), then walk it off heading to the **Flannery O'Connor Childhood Home** (p114) or the nearby **Cathedral of St John the Baptist** (p115; pictured above).

Dinner is upscale Southern classics at Planter's Tavern in the basement of the **Olde Pink House** (p117). Finally, catch a ghost tour at **Sorrel Weed House** (p114) and enjoy some cocktails next door at **Artillery** (p118).

Day 4, Savannah

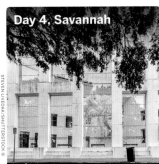

Start the day with a dose of fine art at the **Telfair Academy** (p114) and the **Jepson Center** (p114; pictured above), then get a little retail therapy along West Broughton St.

For lunch, try a twist on classic diner favorites at **Little Duck** (p117), then check out the **American Prohibition Museum** (p115). Make your way across Bay St and down the steep staircases leading to the cobbled River St, where you can watch container ships headed in and out to sea on the Savannah River.

Enjoy inspired Southern comfort food favorites at **The Grey** (p117), a bus station turned retro-chic restaurant, then wander back across MLK Blvd and spend the night bar hopping down Congress St.

Need to Know

For detailed information, see Survival Guide p147

Cell Phones
International travelers can use local SIM cards in an unlocked smartphone or buy a cheap US phone and load it up with prepaid minutes.

Currency
US$

Languages
English, Gullah

Money
ATMs are widespread, and credit cards are accepted almost everywhere.

Time
Eastern Standard Time (GMT/UTC minus five hours)

Tipping
A 15 to 18% tip is expected in restaurants for a job well done.

Visas
Be sure you meet all ESTA visa requirements for travel to the US.

Daily Budget

Budget: Less than $165
Room at a chain motel: $135
BBQ sandwich: $10
Pint of beer: $6

Midrange: $165–275
Room at a historic hotel: $225
Bowl of shrimp and grits: $20
A well-liquor mint julep: $8

Top end: More than $275
Room at a Victorian B&B: $350
Steak dinner: $35
Craft cocktail: $15

Advance Planning

Three to nine months before Make reservations for a room at a top hotel and for top restaurants.

One month before Check online listings for upcoming theater, music and comedy performances, especially for peak months.

One week before Decide on tours and book tickets. Some require a minimum number of people, so nail down the right one in advance rather than just showing up.

Arriving in Charleston & Savannah

Most visitors arrive by air or with their own wheels. It's also possible to take a bus or a train.

✈ Charleston International Airport

Twenty minutes northwest of the city.
Shuttle $3.50-14, **Taxi** $25-30, **Bus** $2, **Rideshare** $17

✈ Savannah/Hilton Head International Airport

Twenty minutes northwest of the city.
Shuttle free-$28, **Taxi** $28, **Bus** $8

Getting Around

Bicycles, boats, buses, rental cars and taxis are all available in Savannah and Charleston.

🚲 Bicycle

Bike-share stations, rental shops and racks are plentiful.

🚌 Bus

In Charleston, city buses cost $2 a ride, and there's also a free streetcar that makes loops from the visitor center.

In Savannah, Chatham Area Transit (www.catchacat.org) operates bio-diesel buses, including a free shuttle (the 'dot') in the Historic District.

⚓ Boat

A ferry service makes four stops around Charleston Harbor.

The free Savannah Belles Ferry (www.catchacat.org; pictured below) connects downtown with Hutchinson Island.

🚗 Car & Motorcycle

Transportation by car is the easiest and most used means of getting around.

🚗 Taxi

Ridesharing apps are usually cheaper and easier than calling or finding taxis.

Charleston Neighborhoods

East Side, NoMo & Hampton Park (p45)
Historic sights abound in these quiet neighborhoods.

Harleston Village, Upper King & Cannonborough Elliotborough (p61)
Stumble across offbeat museums and galleries as you wander.

Aiken-Rhett House ⊙

⊙ Old Slave Mart Museum

McLeod Plantation ⊙

⊙ Fort Sumter National Monument

Charleston County Sea Islands (p77)
Plantations, historic sites and lots of beaches.

South of Broad & the French Quarter (p31)
Home to many of downtown Charleston's best sights, these neighborhoods ooze charm and quiet elegance.

Savannah Neighborhoods

Historic District & Forsyth Park (p107)
The monuments, museums and grand homes of the Historic District will keep you wandering in wonder.

Beaufort & Hilton Head Island (p95)
Connect with the history and culture of colonial Beaufort before exploring 12 miles' worth of beaches on Hilton Head Island.

Forsyth Park

Bonaventure Cemetery

Laurel Grove Cemetery

Wormsloe Historic Site

East Savannah & the Islands (p135)
This stretch of coastal Savannah is a sight in and of itself.

Midtown & the Victorian District (p123)
Astounding residential architecture and a vibrant arts community.

Explore
Charleston & Savannah

Charleston

South of Broad & the French Quarter 31

East Side, NoMo & Hampton Park 45

Harleston Village, Upper King &
Cannonborough Elliotborough 61

Charleston County Sea Islands 77

Beaufort & Hilton Head Island................... 95

Charleston's Walking Tours 🥾

South of Broad 34

Hampton Park 48

Cannonborough Elliotborough 62

Savannah

Historic District & Forsyth Park 107

Midtown & the Victorian District............. 123

East Savannah & the Islands.................... 135

Savannah's Walking Tours 🥾

Savannah's Squares...110

Worth a Trip

Fort Sumter National Monument 90

Wormsloe Historic Site..144

Savannah's Historic District (p107) F11PHOTO/SHUTTERSTOCK ©

Explore
South of Broad & the French Quarter

The storybook Southern charm of the peninsula's southeastern tip cannot be exaggerated. South of Broad is simply awash in quiet elegance, and has long been considered the zenith of Charlestonian prosperity. In the French Quarter, romance emanates from cobblestone streets, and the city's oldest buildings perch among delicious restaurants and vibrant galleries.

In South of Broad the most interesting historic homes (also known as urban plantations) include the Heyward-Washington House (p38), the Nathaniel Russell House (p38) and the Edmondston-Alston House (p39). The Calhoun Mansion (p38) is postbellum, but this Gilded Age manor is the most ostentatious property in all of Charleston. The French Quarter's top attraction is the Old Slave Mart Museum (p32), and the neighborhood also lends itself to a looser itinerary of grabbing cocktail on rooftops, dipping into galleries and admiring centuries-old churches.

Getting There & Around

South of Broad and the French Quarter are easily navigated on foot, though you must watch where you're going (the sidewalks can be uneven). A couple of CARTA (p151) public bus routes serve these neighborhoods, and Charleston's bike share program Holy Spokes (p150) has stations around the area.

South of Broad & French Quarter Map on p36

Rainbow Row (p40) GORDON BELL/SHUTTERSTOCK ©

Top Sight 📷
Old Slave Mart Museum

Formerly called Ryan's Mart, this building once housed an open-air market that auctioned African American men, women and children in the mid-1800s, the largest of 40 or so similar auction houses. South Carolina's shameful past is unraveled in text-heavy exhibits illuminating the slave experience; the few artifacts, such as leg shackles, are especially chilling.

◎ MAP P36, C3

📞 843-958-6467

www.oldslavemart.org

6 Chalmers St

adult/child 5-17yr $8/5

🕒 9am-5pm Mon-Sat

Visiting the Museum

Before you start visiting Charleston's historic homes and plantations, and before you start walking the charming city streets, it's a good idea to educate yourself on why the area thrived before the Civil War. The short answer is: slave labor drove the economy and essentially built the city. Charleston was the nation's slave trade capital, and millions of enslaved people entered the country via the port of Charleston.

Set inside a former slave auction house known as Ryan's Mart, the Old Slave Mart Museum offers a no-holds-barred look at the business of the slave trade. Within its brick walls you'll hear the voices and the stories of enslaved people, and you'll see the shackles they wore, the whips they were beaten with and even a deed of sale for auctioned slaves.

The museum consists of just a few exhibits and text-heavy displays spread over the 1st and 2nd floors of the small building, so it'll only take an hour or two. For firsthand stories, listen to the oral recollections of former slave Elijah Green and others. In a word: haunting.

The importance of this sight looms large in the historical context of Charleston, South Carolina, the United States and beyond.

Don't Miss

o Firsthand accounts of the slave trade from freed slaves.

o A deed of sale for 235 enslaved people.

★ **Top Tips**

o Around Charleston you can find bricks with fingerprints belonging to the enslaved. Ask a docent to show you some here.

o As you wander the museum, keep in mind that you're standing in the place where traders sold human beings who were born into slavery.

✗ **Take a Break**

The museum is heavy, and many visitors come out needing to discuss the content with loved ones or to recharge a bit.

Grab a drink in the courtyard of the nearby Blind Tiger (p41).

Pick up some local moonshine at the Tavern at Rainbow Row (p43).

Walking Tour 🥾

South of Broad

You've got quite a lot of sights to hit, not to mention all the trappings of history peppered throughout the neighborhood: the old-world gas lanterns, the bricks exposed behind peeling stucco, and the 18th-century cannons jutting out of the sidewalks. This itinerary lines up the attractions and unrelenting charm in a logical way, with plenty of time for poking around palatial historic homes and peering through wrought-iron gates at flourishing gardens.

Walk Facts

Start Old Exchange & Provost Dungeon

End Four Corners of Law/ St Michael's Church (intersection of Meeting and Broad Sts)

Length 1½ miles; one hour

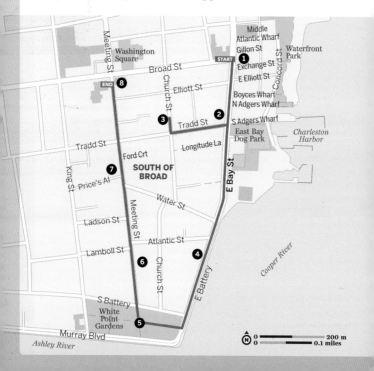

❶ Old Exchange & Provost Dungeon

Begin at the **Old Exchange & Provost Dungeon** (p39), where costumed guides lead tours of the dungeon where Stede Bonnet, the Gentleman Pirate, and Revolutionary War prisoners were once imprisoned.

❷ Rainbow Row

Head south to the picturesquely pastel **Rainbow Row** (p40), where you can snap your shot of these re-done 1730s merchant stores that inspired the birth of the Charleston Preservation Society, along with a restoration of the entire city in the 1920s.

❸ Heyward-Washington House

On Church St, take a right and the **Heyward-Washington House** (p38), where the first president shacked up in 1791, will be on your left.

❹ Edmondston-Alston House

Head along East Battery to the Federal-style **Edmondston-Alston House** (p39), where a docent-led tour brings guests through the public rooms to view intricate woodwork and family artifacts.

❺ Battery & White Point Garden

Continue south to approach the **Battery & White Point Garden**
(p40), named for the fortifications that used to line the seafront and for the mounds of oyster shells once piled over the point.

❻ Calhoun Mansion

Cut through the park and make your way north along Meeting St to the **Calhoun Mansion** (p38), a Gilded Age manor and Charleston's largest single family residence. It overflows with over-the-top souvenirs from the eccentric owner's far-flung travels.

❼ Nathaniel Russell House

Continuing north, the **Nathaniel Russell House** (p38) will appear on the left, and a tour here is worthwhile for its square-oval-rectangle footprint and free-flying spiral staircase. Don't miss the joggling board in the yard.

❽ St Michael's Church

At your final stop, the Four Corners of Law, notice **St Michael's Church** (📞843-723-0603; http://stmichaelschurch.net; 71 Broad St) on the southeast corner, representing God's law. St Michael's is the oldest church in town, and its bells have been announcing earthquakes, hurricanes, fires and attacks on the city for more than 250 years.

✕ Take a Break

Pick up a yummy sandwich at **Brown Dog Deli** (p41).

South of Broad & the French Quarter

HISTORIC DISTRICT

ANSONBOROUGH

FRENCH QUARTER

Waterfront Park

Waterfront Park

400 m
0.2 miles

Concord St

Cumberland St

E Bay St

State St

Queen St

Church St

Meeting St

King St

Vendue Range

Prioleau St

Middle Atlantic Wharf

Boyces Wharf

E Elliott St

Elliott St

Broad St

Chalmers St

Washington Square

St Michaels Al

Jacobs Al

Hortbeck Al

Queen St

St Phillips Church

West Cemetery

Charleston Footprints

Hayne St

Church St

Anson St

N Market St
S Market St

Linguard St

Pinckney St

Beaufain St

Market St
Princess St
Fulton St

Hasell St

Guigand St

Bulldog Tours

Old Slave Mart Museum

5 Old Exchange & Provost Dungeon

Concord St

E Bay St

9 ⊗
12 ⊗
14
11 ⊗
17
15
18
16
19
10 ⊗
13
20
21
8 ⊗

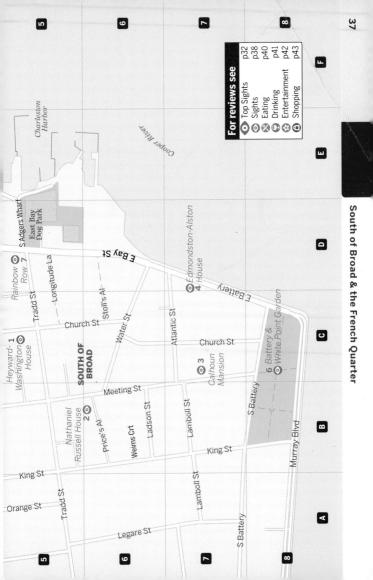

South of Broad & the French Quarter

For reviews see

◎ Top Sights   p32
◎ Sights   p38
✗ Eating   p40
🍸 Drinking   p41
✦ Entertainment   p42
🛍 Shopping   p43

Charleston Harbor

Cooper River

S Adgers Wharf

East Bay Dog Park

Rainbow Row 7

Heyward-Washington House

Longitude La

Tradd St

Church St

Stoll's Al

Water St

E Bay St

SOUTH OF BROAD

Nathaniel Russell House 2

Price's Al

Meeting St

Weims Crt

Ladson St

Atlantic St

Church St

Edmondston-Alston House 4

E Battery

3

Calhoun Mansion

Lamboll St

King St

S Battery

Battery & White Point Garden 6

Murray Blvd

King St

Tradd St

Orange St

Lamboll St

Legare St

S Battery

Sights

Heyward-Washington House
HISTORIC BUILDING

1 ◉ MAP P36, C5

As the name hints, this 1772 Georgian-style town house is kind of a big deal because George Washington rented it for a week, and visitors can stand in what was likely his bedroom. The owner, Thomas Heyward, Jr, was one of South Carolina's four signers of the Declaration of Independence, and it's fun to think about all the talk of revolution that must have taken place in the withdrawing room.

Enthusiasts of old-timey furnishings will appreciate the collection here, which includes a chair that belonged to General Francis Marion (the 'Swamp Fox') and the priceless Holmes bookcase, which was declared on *Antiques Roadshow* to be the most magnificent piece of furniture in America. (☏843-722-0354; www.charleston museum.org; 87 Church St; adult $12, child 13-17yr/3-12yr $10/5; ◷10am-5pm Mon-Sat, noon-5pm Sun)

Nathaniel Russell House
HISTORIC BUILDING

2 ◉ MAP P36, B6

A spectacular, self-supporting spiral staircase is the highlight at this 1808 Federal-style house, built by a Rhode Islander, known in Charleston as 'King of the Yankees.' A meticulous ongoing restoration honors the home to the finest details, such as the 1000 sheets of 22-karat gold leaf in the withdrawing room. Twenty layers of wall paint were peeled back to uncover the original colors, and handmade, fitted, contoured rugs were imported from the UK, as originally done by the Russells.

The small but lush English garden is also notable, as is the square-oval-rectangle footprint of the home. (☏843-724-8481; www. historiccharleston.org; 51 Meeting St; adult/child 6-16yr $12/5; ◷10am-5pm, last tour 4:30pm)

Calhoun Mansion
MUSEUM

3 ◉ MAP P36, C7

If you've ever wondered what the wealthiest, fanciest, most well-traveled hoarder's house might look like, visit the Calhoun Mansion. With 35 rooms and 24,000 sq ft, this Gilded Age, Italianate manor is Charleston's largest single family residence, and nearly every inch of it brims with the eccentric homeowner's collected furnishings, art and antiques from around the world.

Many visitors find it gaudy, but collectors often salivate, and everybody's jaws tend to drop at the sight of the Imperial Russian malachite table, the red sofa that belonged to Napoleon's brother, the hippopotamus-tooth chandelier, the samurai warrior replica that dates back to the Ming dynasty and folds into a carrying case – you get the idea. (☏843-722-8205; www.calhounmansion.net; 16 Meeting St; $17; ◷11am-5pm)

Edmondston-Alston House

HISTORIC BUILDING

4 👁 MAP P36, D7

Charles Edmondston built this Federal-style home in 1825 for a mere $25,000, and fell on hard times in 1837, forcing him to sell it to Charles Alston for $15,500. The Alston family upgraded the home in Greek Revival style, and it remains in their possession, with one member continuing to reside on the 3rd floor. A couple of other rooms and a carriage house out back operate as a high-end B&B.

The docent-led tour brings guests through the public rooms, which feature intricate woodwork, family artifacts and an original print of the Ordinance of Secession. The 2nd floor and piazza are ideal spots to view the harbor. (📞843-722-7171; www.edmondston alston.com; 21 E Battery; adult/child 6-16yr $12/6; 🕐1-4:30pm Sun & Mon, 10:30am-4:30pm Tue-Sat)

Old Exchange & Provost Dungeon

HISTORIC BUILDING

5 👁 MAP P36, D4

Kids love the creepy dungeon, used as a prison for American patriots held by the British during the Revolutionary War. The cramped space sits beneath a stately Georgian Palladian customs house completed in 1771. Costumed guides lead the dungeon tours. Exhibits about the city are displayed on the upper floors.

Combination tickets with the Old Slave Mart Museum cost

Old Exchange & Provost Dungeon

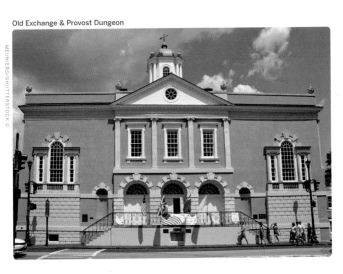

Walking Tours

Charleston Footprints
(Map p36, B3; 843-478-4718;
www.charlestonfootprints.com;
2hr tour $20) offers an excellent walking tour of historical
sights led by a knowledgeable
and theatrical local. **Bulldog
Tours** (Map p36, C1; 843-722-8687; https://bulldogtours.com;
18 Anson St; ghost tour adult/
child $25/15) also has fantastic
guides for this neighborhood.

adult/child $15/8. (843-727-2165;
www.oldexchange.org; 122 E Bay St;
adult/7-12yr $10/5; 9am-5pm;)

Battery & White Point Garden GARDENS

6 MAP P36, C8

The Battery is the southern tip of
the Charleston Peninsula, buffered
by a seawall. Stroll past cannons
and statues of military heroes in
the gardens, then walk the promenade and look for Fort Sumter.
(cnr East Battery & Murray Blvd)

Rainbow Row AREA

7 MAP P36, D5

With its 13 candy-colored houses,
this stretch of Georgian row houses
on lower E Bay St is one of the most
photographed areas in Charleston.
The structures date back to 1730,
when they served as merchant
stores on the wharf, a sketchy part
of town at the time. Starting in the

1920s the buildings were restored
and painted over in pastels. People
dug it, and soon much of the rest
of Charleston was getting a similar
makeover. (83 E Bay St)

Eating

Gaulart & Maliclet FRENCH $

8 MAP P36, B4

Ooh la la. Locals crowd around
the shared tables at this tiny spot,
known as 'Fast & French,' to nibble
on Gallic cheeses and sausages,
fondues or nightly specials ($21 to
$24) that include soup, a main dish
and wine. (843-577-9797; www.
fastandfrenchcharleston.com; 98 Broad
St; breakfast $5-11, lunch & dinner mains
$11-14; 8am-4pm Mon, to 10pm Tue-
Thu, to 10:30pm Fri & Sat)

Fleet Landing SEAFOOD $$

9 MAP P36, E2

Come here for the perfect Charleston lunch: a river view, a cup of
she-crab soup with a splash of
sherry, and a big bowl of shrimp
and grits. Housed in a former naval
degaussing building on a pier, it's a
convenient and scenic spot to enjoy
fresh fish, a fried seafood platter or
a burger after a morning of downtown exploring.

Smothered in tasso-ham gravy,
the shrimp and grits here look dirty,
not highfalutin, and they're our
favorite version in the city. (843-
722-8100; www.fleetlanding.net; 186
Concord St; lunch mains $9-24, dinner
mains $13-26; 11am-3:30pm daily,
5-10pm Sun-Thu, 5-11pm Fri & Sat;)

Brown Dog Deli

SANDWICHES $

10 MAP P36, C4

Really tasty gourmet sandwiches, packed with fresh and creative ingredients. A favorite is the Boar's Head mesquite turkey with a brie spread, bacon, sprouts, red onions and cranberry-pepper jelly. The salads and wraps are also worthwhile, and there's a second location over on the corner of Calhoun and Smith Sts. (☑843-853-8081; www.browndogdeli.com; 40 Broad St; sandwiches $8-14; ☺11am-6pm Mon-Thu, to 8pm Fri & Sat, to 4pm Sun)

Minero

TACOS $

11 MAP P36, D3

James Beard Award–winning chef and Charleston darling Sean Brock is behind this vibrant and affordable Mexican joint. The food to get is the tacos, which involve inventive, flavorful combos like catfish and pickled green-tomato tartar or grilled cauliflower and salsa macha. There's a long, awesome tequila list, too. (☑843-789-2241; http://minerorestaurant.com/charleston; 153b E Bay St; tacos from $4.50; ☺11am-10pm Sun-Thu, to 11pm Fri & Sat)

Slightly North of Broad

SOUTHERN US $$$

12 MAP P36, D2

A tried-and-true French Quarter mainstay, with a rotating menu of Lowcountry comfort dishes reinvented with flair. Best bets include the peach salad (served with prosciutto, goat's cheese and pecans) and the duck breast. The management group behind Halls Chophouse (p69) took over this place in 2016 and left everything exactly as it was. (SNOB; ☑843-723-3424; http://snobcharleston.com; 192 E Bay St; mains $28-36; ☺11:30am-2:30pm & 5pm-late Mon-Sat, 10:30am-2pm & 5pm-late Sun)

Drinking

Blind Tiger

PUB

13 MAP P36, C4

Opened in 1893, this cozy and atmospheric former dive, reborn in 2016 after an extensive restoration, seduces with stamped-tin ceilings, good pub grub and barrels of history. The expansive back courtyard is a popular place for a blind mule cocktail, which comes with vodka, ginger beer, lime juice and a candied ginger garnish. (www.blindtigerchs.com; 36-38 Broad St; ☺11am-2am)

Joggling Boards

You are not a true Charlestonian unless you have a joggling board, and South of Broad is the epicenter for this absurd but delightful porch furnishing. It consists of a 16ft plank set on rockers, and was apparently used in the early 1800s to cure rheumatoid arthritis and aid in courtship. You can find one in the yard of the Nathaniel Russell House.

Rooftop at the Vendue BAR

14 🕐 MAP P36, D3

This rooftop bar has sweet views of downtown and the crowds to prove it. Enjoy craft cocktails, and live music on Sundays from 2pm to 5pm. (www.thevendue.com; 23 Vendue Range; ⏰11:30am-10pm Sun-Thu, to midnight Fri & Sat)

Pavilion Bar ROOFTOP BAR

15 🕐 MAP P36, D1

Complete with an infinity pool, illuminated umbrellas and stunning city views, this swanky rooftop bar tends to attract a well-heeled set. But people sometimes end up barefoot when the hotel throws plexiglass over the pool and converts it into a dance floor. (📞843-723-0500; www.marketpavilion.com; 225 E Bay St; cocktails from $9; ⏰11:30am-midnight)

Entertainment

Dock Street Theatre THEATER

16 ⭐ MAP P36, C3

Dock Street Theatre is an exquisite place to see theater. It has plenty of history – a previous iteration opened in 1736 on the same spot, becoming the first theater in America. The current performing arts center is also historic; it was built in 1809 and first occupied by the Planter's Hotel. Today it's the last (former) hotel from the antebellum period. Its Regency-style facade looks like it's straight out of New Orleans, and the wrought-iron balcony and brownstone columns channel

Charleston City Market

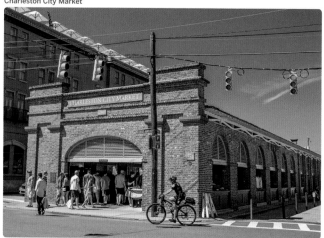

FILIPHOTO/SHUTTERSTOCK ©

the 1800s. It's now home to the Charleston Stage Company, and also contains the city's Cultural Affairs office and the City Gallery. (📞843-720-3968; www.charleston stage.com; 135 Church St)

Shopping

Robert Lange Studios ART

17 🔒 MAP P36, D3

Some of the city's best contemporary art regularly appears in this long-standing downtown gallery. Artist Nathan Durfee's experimental work is a highlight, and during **ArtWalk** (📞304-340-4253; www.artwalkcw.com; ⏱5-8pm third Thu of the month, usually) it is a madhouse. (📞843-805-8052; http://robertlange studios.com; 2 Queen St; ⏱11am-5pm)

Charleston City Market MARKET

18 🔒 MAP P36, C1

With more than 300 vendors hawking everything from sweetgrass baskets to piping-hot biscuits, this vibrant, open-air market is one of the nation's oldest, getting its start in 1804. The night market is held in the same space and runs from April to December, displaying the wares of more than 100 local artists and craftspeople. (📞843-937-0920; www.thecharleston citymarket.com; 188 Meeting St; ⏱day market 9:30am-6pm year-round, night market 6:30-10:30pm Fri & Sat Apr-Dec)

National Register of Historic Places

There are 190 properties and districts in Charleston County on the National Register of Historic Places, the federal government's official list of places deemed worthy of preservation.

Shops of Historic Charleston Foundation GIFTS & SOUVENIRS

19 🔒 MAP P36, B3

This place showcases jewelry, home furnishings and furniture inspired by the city's historic homes. (📞843-724-8484; www.historiccharleston.org; 108 Meeting St; ⏱9am-6pm Mon-Sat, noon-5pm Sun)

Tavern at Rainbow Row ALCOHOL

20 🔒 MAP P36, D4

America's oldest liquor store has been getting people drunk since 1686. There are free tastings of local whiskey and moonshine on weekends. (📞843-722-4800; www.charlestonspirits.com; 120 E Bay St; ⏱10am-7pm Mon-Sat)

W Hampton Brand Gallery ARTS & CRAFTS

21 🔒 MAP P36, D4

An excellent place to unearth unique souvenirs and gifts, such as likenesses of the homes of Rainbow Row, painted on reclaimed slate roof tiles. (📞843-327-6282; 114 E Bay St; ⏱9am-2pm Thu-Mon)

Explore ⬡
East Side, NoMo & Hampton Park

Away from most of the tourist hubbub, the northern and eastern stretches of Charleston are fairly quiet, with a few noteworthy attractions. The East Side features a number of top restaurants, some off-the-beaten-track inns and a jumping-off point for Fort Sumter (p90). NoMo (North Morrison) was once industrial but has more recently attracted some tech companies and decent restaurants. Hampton Park, while primarily residential, offers expansive green spaces and some hyper-local cafes and breweries.

Most of the must-see sights in these neighborhoods are clustered on the East Side and tend to be historical in nature (the Aiken-Rhett House (p46), the Charleston Museum (p52) and the Joseph Manigault House (p52) are all top notch). The South Carolina Aquarium (p52) is great for kids. The Hampton Park area offers less-visited sights including the Citadel (p53) and Hampton Park (p52).

Getting There & Around
Walking these neighborhoods is possible, but some attractions are a bit spread out, making wheels more convenient. A couple of public bus routes run here, and the water taxi connects Aquarium Wharf on the East Side to Patriot's Point, Charleston Harbor Resort and Waterfront Park. Charleston's bike-share program has stations around the area.

East Side, NoMo & Hampton Park Map on p50

Hampton Park (p52) CVANDYKE/SHUTTERSTOCK ©

Top Sight 📷
Aiken-Rhett House

*The only surviving urban town-house complex,
this 1820 abode gives a fascinating glimpse
into antebellum life on a 45-minute self-guided
audio tour. The role of slaves is emphasized and
visitors wander into their dorm-style quarters
before moving on to the lifestyle of the rich and
famous. The Historic Charleston Foundation has
conserved but not restored the home, so you get
the peeling Parisian wallpaper and all.*

◎ MAP P50, F4

📞 843-723-1159

www.historiccharleston.
org

48 Elizabeth St

adult/child 6-16yr $12/5

🕐 10am-5pm, last tour
4:15pm

Main House

Stepping through the ornate doors of this tangerine-colored mansion feels a bit like time-traveling to 1858. Not much has changed inside former South Carolina Governor William Aiken's home, and the collection of books, furnishings, art and architectural details, though worn, is largely intact. Some will find it a bit too *Great Expectations,* others will simply enjoy gawking at the peeling wallpaper, cracked plaster and chamber pots.

A stroll through the home offers insight into evolving architectural tastes in the first half of the 19th century. The upper floors exemplify the late Federal period with their careful woodwork and symmetrical proportions, while the main floor and marble staircase have been renovated in the Greek Revival style. The art gallery added in 1858 recalls the Victorian era.

Slave Quarters

The Aiken-Rhett House is often referred to as an urban plantation, and it's no secret that enslaved people lived and toiled away here as cooks, laundresses, footmen, seamstresses, gardeners and the like. Fourteen slaves are thought to have occupied the cramped 2nd-story quarters at the back of the home, and to have shared a communal kitchen. Careful analysis has suggested that the rooms had fireplaces and were painted in bright colors.

An archaeological dig in the property's laundry room has yielded some promising finds, including egg shells, fish scales, bottles, pottery and ceramics. The items (numbering more than 10,000 in total) offer insight into the daily lives of the enslaved, and some are on display.

Courtyard

Wandering the walled courtyard of the Aiken-Rhett House is an adventure, with a couple of key highlights.

★ Top Tips

○ Get a combo ticket for both the Aiken-Rhett House and the Nathaniel Russell House for $18, which saves you $6 (you have six months to visit both).

○ Store bags in free lockers while touring.

○ Pause the audio headset and linger when you feel compelled, or just turn it off and wander a while.

✗ Take a Break

King St is just a couple of blocks away, with plenty of snacking and drinking options.

Callie's Hot Little Biscuit (☎ 843-737-5159; http://callies biscuits.com; 476 1/2 King St; biscuit sandwiches $7; ⊙7am-2pm Mon-Fri, from 8am Sat & Sun, 10pm-2am Fri & Sat) offers the quintessential Charleston snack.

Juanita Greenberg's Nacho Royale (p68) has – you guessed it – amazing nachos.

Walking Tour 🚶

Hampton Park

With oodles of green space and the occasional neighborhood watering hole, sleepy Hampton Park is an ideal 'hood for a lazy Sunday stroll. Those that reside in the early-1900s abodes here tend to be raising children or part of the military, but many further-flung Charlestonians descend regularly to chillax in the grass, watch baseball or patronize their favorite bars.

Walk Facts

Start Revelry Brewery

End Palmetto Brewing Company

Duration Two hours

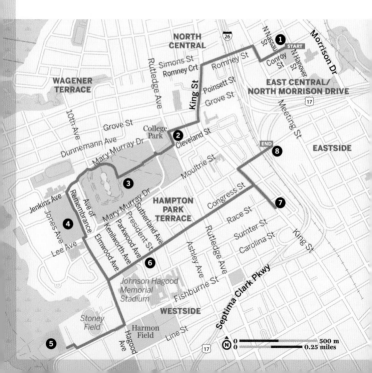

❶ Revelry Brewery

Revelry Brewery (p56) is a top spot for throwing back local craft beer on a rooftop, surrounded by locals and their dogs. Fridays and Saturdays are especially bumpin', and there's usually live music.

❷ Moe's Crosstown Tavern

Hands down the most popular sports dive in Charleston, **Moe's Crosstown Tavern** (p56) is famous for Sunday brunch, burgers and game-day festivities. Here people will treat you like you've been their friend for a decade.

❸ Hampton Park

Hampton Park (p52) is Charleston's largest green space, and it sure is pretty. Locals flock here every weekend to enjoy the gardens, Frisbee matches and wide-open expanses of controlled nature.

❹ Citadel

In its own little world, the **Citadel** (p53) offers a surprisingly attractive campus, innumerable cadets in uniform and a small museum featuring military apparel. Even if war isn't your thing, the center of the complex is mostly manicured lawns.

❺ The Joe

Otherwise known as **Joseph P Riley, Jr Park** (p59), this baseball stadium fills with RiverDogs fans in the spring and summer months. And apparently the food here is surprisingly tasty.

❻ Harold's Cabin

Bill Murray is the ultimate local, and he part-owns **Harold's Cabin** (p55), a former corner store turned hipster haunt with locally sourced grocery items, jackalope art, a restaurant and a bar.

❼ Leon's Oyster Shop

True locals do **Leon's Oyster Shop** (p54) on Saturday, and then again on Sunday. The oysters, scalloped potatoes and fried chicken are really that good. It gets bonus points for being set inside a converted old body shop.

❽ Palmetto Brewing Company

You might as well bookend your journey with breweries, and **Palmetto Brewing Company** (p57) is the place to end up. It was the city's first microbrewery and still holds a place in every Charlestonian's heart.

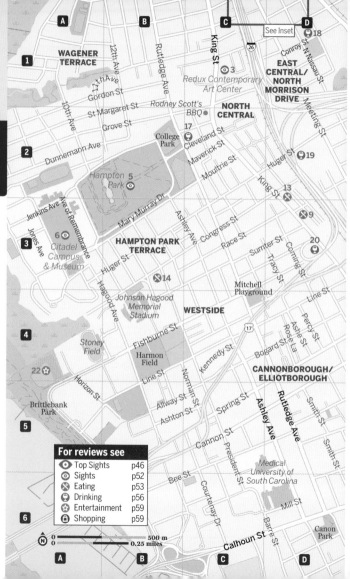

WAGENER TERRACE

12th Ave

11th Ave
Gordon St
10th Ave
St Margaret St
Grove St
Dunnemann Ave

Rutledge Ave

King St

26

EAST CENTRAL/ NORTH MORRISON DRIVE

Conroy St
N Nassau St

18

See Inset

3 Redux Contemporary Art Center

Rodney Scott's BBQ

NORTH CENTRAL

17
College Park
Cleveland St
Maverick St
Moultrie St

Meeting St

Huger St

19

Hampton Park 5

Mary Murray Dr

Ashley Ave

Congress St

King St

13

9

Ave of Remembrance
Jenkins Ave
Jones Ave

6
Citadel Campus & Museum

Huger St

HAMPTON PARK TERRACE

Race St

Sumter St

Tracy St

Coming St

20

Hagood Ave

14

Johnson Hagood Memorial Stadium

WESTSIDE

Mitchell Playground

Line St

17

Ashe St
Rose La

Percy St

Stoney Field

Fishburne St

Harmon Field

22

Horizon St

Line St

Kennedy St

Norman St

CANNONBOROUGH/ ELLIOTBOROUGH

Rutledge Ave

Smith St

Smith St

Brittlebank Park

Allway St

Ashton St

Spring St

Cannon St

Ashley Ave

Smith St

President St

Bee St

Courtenay Dr

Medical University of South Carolina

Mill St

Canon Park

Calhoun St

For reviews see
⊙ Top Sights   p46
⊙ Sights   p52
⊗ Eating   p53
◯ Drinking   p56
☆ Entertainment   p59
⌂ Shopping   p59

N
0   500 m
0   0.25 miles

A   B   C   D

E   F   G   H

Morrison Dr

Newmarket Creek

17

Johnson St

Inset

23

24

10

12

Morrison Dr

**EAST CENTRAL/
NORTH
MORRISON DRIVE**

Meeting St

Brigade St

William St

Lewis
Barbecue

N Hanover St

N Isabella St

N Nassau St

26

0   200 m
0   0.1 miles

E Bay St

Lee St

Martins
Park

EASTSIDE

Hanover St

America St

Harris St

Nassau St

Jackson St

Lee St

Cooper St

Aiken St

Blake St

America St

Hanover St

Meeting St

Columbus St

Hampstead
Mall
Playground

Drake St

Spring St   8

Nassau St

Amherst St

Reid St

South St

Woolfe St

King St

Cannon St

Callie's
Hot Little
Biscuit

Wragg Sq

Mary St

**Aiken-Rhett
House** 1

**MAZYCK-
WRAGGBOROUGH**

E Bay St

Cooper River

South Carolina
Aquarium 2

Fort Sumter
Boat Tour

Morris St

St Philip St

Coming St

Radcliffe St

**Charleston
Museum** 1

John St

Joseph
Manigault House 4

Elizabeth St

Charlotte St

Alexander St

Aquarium Wharf/
Maritime Center

Warren St

RADCLIFFBOROUGH

Vanderhorst St

Hutson St

Marion
Square

Calhoun St

15

ANSONBOROUGH

Laurens St

Washington St

Calhoun St

Smith St

Pitt St

Bull St

**HARLESTON
VILLAGE**

College of
Charleston

Glebe St

St Philip St

King St

**HISTORIC
DISTRICT**

George St

Society St

21

Wentworth St

Anson St

7

E Bay St

Hasell St

16

11

Old South Carriage Co

Culinary Tours
of Charleston

Sights

Charleston Museum   MUSEUM

1 ⊙ MAP P50, F5

Founded in 1773, this is the country's oldest museum. It's helpful and informative if you're looking for historical background before strolling through the Historic District. Exhibits spotlight various periods of Charleston's long and storied history.

Artifacts include a whale skeleton, slave tags and the 'secession table' used for the signing of the state's secession documents. And don't miss Charleston's polar bear. (☎843-722-2996; www.charleston museum.org; 360 Meeting St; adult $12, child 13-17yr/3-12yr $10/5; ☉9am-5pm Mon-Sat, noon-5pm Sun)

South Carolina Aquarium   AQUARIUM

2 ⊙ MAP P50, H4

A showcase of South Carolina's wildlife, with creatures hailing from the mountain forest, piedmont, salt marsh, coastal and undersea habitats. Although the facility is rather small in comparison with some of the country's more prominent aquariums, there are plenty of fish and other creatures. Noteworthy residents include otters, rattlesnakes, sharks and an albino alligator.

A newly upgraded sea turtle rehabilitation wing is a huge hit with both kids and adults. (☎843-577-3474; http://scaquarium.org; 100 Aquarium Wharf; adult/child $30/23; ☉9am-5pm; 👪)

Redux Contemporary Art Center   ARTS CENTER

3 ⊙ MAP P50, C1

A contemporary art hub and event space, with three galleries, a few dozen studios and some classrooms. (☎843-722-0697; www.reduxstudios.org; 1056 King St; ☉10am-6pm Tue-Fri, noon-5pm Sat)

Joseph Manigault House   HISTORIC BUILDING

4 ⊙ MAP P50, F5

This three-story Federal-style house from 1803 was once the showpiece of a French Huguenot rice planter. There's a tiny neoclassical gate temple in the garden and the house is full of 19th-century furnishings from the collection of the Charleston Museum, which runs the site. (☎843-722-2996; www.charlestonmuseum.org; 350 Meeting St; adult $12, child 13-17yr/3-12yr $10/5; ☉10am-5pm Mon-Sat, noon-5pm Sun, last tour 4:30pm)

Hampton Park   PARK

5 ⊙ MAP P50, B2

A big, awesome park that locals love for its arboreal and floral displays, fitness trail and large swaths of open space, often utilized for things like Frisbee matches. It has public restrooms and parking, and is rarely crowded. (☎843-724-7327; 30 Mary Murray Dr)

Citadel Campus & Museum

SCHOOL

6 ◉ MAP P50, A3

South Carolina's military college campus is set in historic buildings and is replete with uniformed cadets and various memorials. There's a small museum on the 3rd floor of the library that displays mostly military apparel. It also has a re-creation of historic barracks. (☎843-953-6845; www.citadel.edu/root; 171 Moultrie St; admission free; ⏰7:30am-10pm Mon-Thu, to 5pm Fri, 9am-3pm Sat, noon-10:30pm Sun)

Eating

167 Raw

SEAFOOD $$

7 ✖ MAP P50, G6

There are no reservations at this tiny hole-in-the-wall that unassumingly serves up the city's best seafood. People wait in lines down the block for the delicious lobster roll, and the tuna burger and sea-scallop po'boy are also off-the-charts toothsome. Oysters arrive fresh daily from Nantucket (where the restaurant runs its very own oyster farm), and the service is truly on point. Great wine selection, too. (☎843-579-4997; http://167raw.com/charleston; 289 E Bay St; oysters $2.75 each, mains $14-27; ⏰11am-10pm Mon-Sat)

Citadel Campus & Museum

Tours

The East Side is a jumping-off point for many of the city's best tours. **Carriage tours** (Map p50, G6; ☎843-723-9712; www.oldsouthcarriage.com; 14 Anson St; adult/child $25/15; ☉after 5:30pm), **food tours** (Map p50, G6; ☎843-727-1100; www.culinarytoursofcharleston. com; 18 Anson St; 2½-hr tour from $60) and **ghost tours** (p40) are among the most popular. The **boats for Fort Sumter National Monument** (p90) leave from Aquarium Wharf.

Tu   FUSION $

8 🍴 MAP P50, E4

From the food geniuses who brought us Xiao Bao Biscuit (p67) comes this fusion place where there are no phones, no spoons and seemingly no rules. The playful, strange menu includes guava, habanero and cheese ice, which blows your mind. It's the kind of place you don't even want to explain to people, because you can't. (www.tu-charleston.com; 430 Meeting St; mains $12-15; ☉5-10pm Mon-Thu, to midnight Fri & Sat)

Leon's Oyster Shop   SOUTHERN US $

9 🍴 MAP P50, D3

In a converted old body shop reimagined as an industrial-chic eatery, Leon's is a Charleston favorite for three distinct and delicious items: oysters, fried chicken and scalloped potatoes. There is no better place to eat off a hangover, and the rosé on tap is a classy way to keep the party going. (☎843-531-6500; http:// leonsoystershop.com; 698 King St; oysters from $1, fried chicken meal $15, scalloped potatoes $5; ☉11am-10pm)

Edmund's Oast   PUB FOOD $$

10 🍴 MAP P50, G1

Occupying a gutted former hardware store in gentrifying NoMo, Charleston's highest-brow brewpub got a fancy new executive chef, Bob Cook, in 2017. The new grub: Southern faves like salt chicken skins, hanger steaks and hot-and-sour tilefish. The drink pairings: 64 taps (eight devoted to cocktails, meads and sherries, and a dozen proprietary craft beers, among other craft offerings).

The menu isn't long on options but is absolutely outstanding on execution and flavors that complement the devoted craft scene here. It's named after an 18th-century rebel brewer. Call it a night! (☎843-727-1145; www.edmundsoast.com; 1081 Morrison Dr; mains $14-29, pints $6-9; ☉4:30-10pm Mon-Thu, to 11pm Fri & Sat, 10am-10pm Sun; 🛜)

FIG   SOUTHERN US $$$

11 🍴 MAP P50, G6

FIG has been a longtime foodie favorite, and it's easy to see why: welcoming staff, efficient but unrushed service and top-notch, sustainably sourced nouvelle

Southern fare from James Beard Award–winner Mike Lata. The six nightly changing dishes embrace what's fresh and local from the sea and local farms and mills. FIG stands for Food is Good. And the gourmets agree.

Reservations well in advance are mandatory, but rogue solos might be able to snag a seat quickly at the communal table or bar. (☏843-805-5900; www.eatatfig. com; 232 Meeting St; mains $30-36; ☺5-10:30pm Mon-Thu, to 11pm Fri & Sat; 🛜)

Martha Lou's   SOUTHERN US $

12 🍴 MAP P50, H1

Some of the city's best soul food comes from this unfancy place, just a pale pink shack in NoMo serving up a few meats on paper plates. The fried chicken is divine, and the chitterlings (pig intestines) are pure Gullah goodness. (☏843-577-9583; http://marthalouskitchen. com; 1068 Morrison Dr; meat & two sides $14; ☺11am-6pm Mon-Sat)

Little Jack's Tavern   BURGERS $

13 🍴 MAP P50, D2

A classy neighborhood cocktail bar and restaurant, with one helluva hamburger (in 2017 Bon Appétit named it one of the top three burgers in America). The butter-soaked bun is toasted just right, and the oversized patty is smothered in a fantastic tangy sauce and savory fried onions. (☏843-531-6868; http://littlejackstavern.com; 710 King St; tavern burger $8; ☺11am-10pm Sun-Thu, to 11pm Fri & Sat)

Harold's Cabin   AMERICAN $$

14 🍴 MAP P50, B3

It goes without saying that if Bill Murray is a co-owner, the place is probably dope. That's the case for this former corner store, which remains a rustic (if newly chic) neighborhood haunt offering locally sourced grocery items – and now it's also a restaurant and bar. The delicious, veggie-driven meals are largely made up of ingredients from a rooftop garden.

But yeah, the steaks and seafood are also super yum. Oh, and jackalopes abound. And there's

BBQ

Maybe it's because barbecue needs a lot of room to be prepared and devoured, but the city's best meat-munching happens in expansive spaces in the northern part of town. In fact, the top two spots are within a half-mile of each other, and whether you're on team **Lewis Barbecue** (Map p50, H2; ☏843-805-9500; https://lewisbarbecue.com; 464 N Nassau St; mains $8-21; ☺11am-10pm Tue-Sun) or team **Rodney Scott's BBQ** (Map p50, C2; ☏843-990-9535; www. rodneyscottsbbq.com; 1011 King St; mains $9-14; ☺11am-9pm) is deeply personal.

a great brunch. And apparently you get a small discount if you wear black? (☏843-793-4440; www.haroldscabin.com; 247 Congress St; mains $8-20; ☺11am-10pm Tue-Fri, 9am-10pm Sat & Sun; 🖉)

Zero Café + Bar
AMERICAN $$$

15 ❌ MAP P50, G5

The kitchen at the Zero George Street hotel (p149) might be diminutive, but the dining experience provided by Food Network celebrity chef Vinson Petrillo is enormously memorable. The chef assumes his diners are intrepid and sends out dainty plates of pressure-cooked octopus, ricotta gnudi (gnocchi-like dumplings) and scallop tartare. Vegetarians are well served with items like cappellacci (stuffed pasta) and rutabaga (swede).

The wine list is small, but the tasting-menu pairings are expertly curated. Cocktails and beer are also available (and a fine idea). (☏843-817-7900; www.zerogeorge.com; 0 George St; 6-course tasting menu with wine $135 per person, $125 for veg; ☺5-10pm Tue-Sun; 🖉)

Cru Cafe
AMERICAN $$

16 ❌ MAP P50, G6

Innovative comfort food, served in a two-story, historic home with a charming porch. This place is beloved for its healthy salads and unusual takes on local specialties, for example, the deeply fried green tomatoes with pork-belly croutons,

sheep's-milk feta and smoky caramel drizzle. The General Tso's Caesar wrap is also a winner. (☏843-534-2434; http://crucafe.com; 18 Pinckney St; mains $10-25; ☺11am-3pm & 5-10pm Tue-Thu, 11am-3pm & 5-11pm Fri & Sat)

Drinking

Moe's Crosstown Tavern
SPORTS BAR

17 🍺 MAP P50, C2

Considered Hampton Park's best dive bar, this place fills with loyal patrons on game days. The burgers and Sunday brunch are tasty; the craft beer and camaraderie are even tastier. (☏843-641-0469; https://moescrosstowntavern.com; 714 Rutledge Ave; ☺11am-2am Mon-Sat, 10:30am-2am Sun)

Revelry Brewery
MICROBREWERY

18 🍺 MAP P50, D1

Probably the hippest of the Northern Peninsula breweries. It's hard to beat knocking back a few artfully crafted cold ones on Revelry's fairy-lit and fire-pit-heated rooftop, which affords expansive views all the way to the cable-stayed Ravenel Bridge. The downstairs bar, seemingly owned by the brewery's black Lab, is 5ft from the tanks.

There's live music on Friday and Sunday. Pets are encouraged. In 2018 an annex behind the brewery was slated to open; it sell bottles and cans and eventually host events and tastings. (www.

Plantations Around Charleston

Three significant plantations line the Ashley River about a 20-minute drive from downtown Charleston. All offer talks and tours concerning the role of slavery (though another, **McLeod Plantation** (p78), located on the northern shores of James Island, is the best for an eye-opening and highly important experience on that topic).

Of the three on the Ashley River, **Drayton Hall** (843-769-2600; www.draytonhall.org; 3380 Ashley River Rd; adult/child $22/10, grounds only $12; 9am-3:30pm Mon-Sat, 11am-3:30pm Sun, last tour 3pm) is the best for history buffs, as it features the oldest plantation house open to the public in America. **Magnolia Plantation** (843-571-1266; www.magnoliaplantation.com; 3550 Ashley River Rd; adult/child 6-10yr $20/10, tours $8; 8am-5:30pm Mar-Oct, to 4:30pm Nov-Feb) has great tours and wild gardens, with a Disney vibe. **Middleton Place** (843-556-6020; www.middletonplace.org; 4300 Ashley River Rd; gardens adult/child 6-13yr $28/10, house-museum tour extra $15, carriage tour $18; 9am-5pm) has the country's oldest, most elegant gardens and a fancy restaurant and hotel. You'll be hard-pressed to find the time to visit all three of these in one day, but you could squeeze in two (allow at least a couple of hours for each). Ashley River Rd is also known as SC 61, which can be reached from downtown Charleston via Hwy 17.

Also popular, **Boone Hall Plantation** (843-884-4371; www.boonehallplantation.com; 1235 Long Point Rd; adult/child 6-12yr $24/12; 8:30am-6:30pm Mon-Sat, noon-5pm Sun early Mar-Aug, shorter hours Sep-Jan) in Mt Pleasant is where celebrities tend to get married, and is a very pretty spot for tourists and families. It's 11 miles from downtown Charleston on Hwy 17N.

revelrybrewingco.com; 10 Conroy St; 4-10pm Mon-Thu, noon-midnight Fri & Sat, noon-10pm Sun)

Palmetto Brewing Company

MICROBREWERY

19 MAP P50, D2

Charleston's first microbrewery (since Prohibition, anyway) produces four main craft beers with fresh barley malts and hops: an amber ale, a pilsner and a couple of IPAs. They've also got rotating special ales and even a 'Brose' radler (shandy). Tours are available on weekdays at 5pm, and the tap room and outdoor beer garden are lively on weekends, particularly Fridays.

In 2017 the business was sold to Catawba Brewing Company, and facility and equipment upgrades were pending at the time of

Booming Charleston

These days, the city of Charleston seems to be out for a joyride in a comfy, high-performance carriage. The carriage is cruising at a breakneck pace, yummy snacks and cocktails are getting passed around, and everybody wants to hop on. Sometimes, though, the carriage gets stuck in traffic. The price of the ride keeps going up, and the very people who got the carriage moving can no longer afford it.

This is, of course, a fairly ridiculous allegory to describe a Charleston that is booming economically, has a great restaurant scene and is attracting all kinds of visitors and new residents. But at the same time, that growth is causing traffic problems and gentrification.

The good news first: thanks to the meticulously preserved history and architecture, burgeoning restaurant scene and dreamy waterfront locale, Charleston is enjoying some of the finest times in its near 350-year history. The city's top industry, tourism, has been growing since 2012, with visitors lately tossing more than $20 billion at the city. In 2017 an estimated six million people showed up to see this peninsula that spans just over 100 sq miles. With all the awards the city has been raking in from top publications, the numbers are likely to continue their upward trajectory.

People are also moving to the city in sky-high numbers. US News & World Report recently identified Charleston as the fifth-fastest growing city (in terms of net migration) in the country, and new developments, restaurant openings and job opportunities have been springing up around the peninsula, particularly in the once industrial, now gentrifying area known as NoMo. Some are calling it Silicon Harbor, though, because the area is poised to become Charleston's tech hub, and interesting new businesses like **Workshop** (📞843-996-4500; https://workshopcharleston.com; 1503 King St; mains from $5; ⊙11am-9pm Mon-Thu, to 10pm Fri & Sat, 10am-9pm Sun) – an experimental food court where chefs can test out fresh ideas – have already set up shop.

Although most residents can appreciate the brisket enchiladas, they're not thrilled about the congested city streets or the new hotel and condo projects. Downtown home prices have climbed steeply, making it tougher for locals to afford to buy. The people working low-income jobs in the service sector and/or living in neighborhoods adjacent to NoMo are being displaced as rents climb. City planners estimate that within 20 years, Charleston's population will double, and some are worried that the character of the city that initially attracted everyone will begin to slip away.

research. (☎843-937-0903; www.
palmettobrewery.com; 289 Huger St;
⏰4-8pm Tue-Thu, noon-10pm Fri &
Sat)

Recovery Room BAR

20 🅿 MAP P50, D3

Not what it sounds like. Instead,
it's a late-night dive that often
swells with college students and
boozy regulars in search of cheap
whiskey. Various theme nights include trivia games, live music and
boccie ball. (☎843-727-0999; www.
recoveryroomtavern.com; 685 King St;
⏰3pm-2am Mon-Sat, noon-2am Sun)

Entertainment

Theatre 99 COMEDY

21 🎭 MAP P50, G6

Performances and classes in
improv comedy. Very funny stuff,
to the point where locals drop in
multiple times a week. (☎843-
853-6687; www.theatre99.com; 280
Meeting St; from $5; ⏰shows 8pm
Wed-Sat, sometimes 10pm)

Joseph P Riley, Jr Park BASEBALL

22 ⚾ MAP P50, A4

Home of the RiverDogs minor
league baseball team and the
Citadel team. The stadium is a
namesake of a long-time former
Charleston mayor who regularly
attends games, but it is more often
referred to as 'the Joe.' On ladies
night anyone wearing a skirt gets

in free, and Bill Murray is a part-
owner of the RiverDogs. (The Joe;
☎843-723-7241; www.riverdogs.com;
360 Fisburne St; ⏰Apr-Sep)

Shopping

Edmund's
Oast Exchange ALCOHOL

Formerly known as Charleston
Beer Exchange, this beer and
wine retail store (see 10 ❌ Map p50,
G1) opened near its parent brewery (p54) in 2017. The two-story
space has more than 1000 different varieties of booze available in
cans, bottles, kegs and growlers.
(☎843-990-9449; 1081 Morrison Dr;
⏰11am-8pm Tue-Sat, noon-5pm Sun)

Goat. Sheep. Cow.
North. CHEESE

23 🧀 MAP P50, G1

A gourmet cheese shop that
triples as a cafe and wine bar. Get
your pasteurized Spanish goat's
milk and thermized Italian sheep's
milk here. (☎843-203-3118; https://
goatsheepcow.com; 804 Meeting St;
⏰11am-9:30pm Mon-Sat)

Indigo Market VINTAGE

24 🔒 MAP P50, G1

One-of-a-kind art, jewelry, furnishings, textiles and other gifts, lots
of it vintage. (☎843-805-4555;
https://indigomarketcharleston.com;
1094 Morrison Dr; ⏰10am-5:30pm
Mon-Sat)

Explore

Harleston Village, Upper King & Cannonborough Elliotborough

These three distinct neighborhoods are core areas for college students, young professionals and families to live, work, play and shop. Harleston Village is the most suburban 'hood, with stately mansions, single houses and small shops, but it's also home to the College of Charleston. Upper King is a narrow, densely packed strip of hit-or-miss restaurants, upscale boutiques and loft-style condos. Cannonborough Elliotborough attracts young creatives and families with its fixed-up Victorians and independent businesses.

Places of worship and off-beat museums and galleries abound in these neighborhoods.

Getting There & Around

These neighborhoods are all designed to be enjoyed on foot, with sidewalks and green spaces aplenty. A couple of CARTA (p151) public bus routes serve this part of the city, and Charleston's bike share program Holy Spokes (p150) also has stations around the area.

Harleston Village, Upper King & Cannonborough Elliotborough Map on p64

Randolph Hall, College of Charleston (p66) LEAMUS/GETTY IMAGES ©

Walking Tour

Cannonborough Elliotborough

This unassuming, quiet neighborhood is home to much of Charleston's creative class, and the small restaurants and galleries that have sprung up to serve them are some of the city's best-kept secrets. The gentrification under way here, while unfortunate for low-income residents, has its perks for wanderers, including some lovely Charleston single houses oriented sideways with dreamy, slanted piazzas.

Walk Facts
Start Ice Bing
End Sugar Bakeshop
Duration Two hours

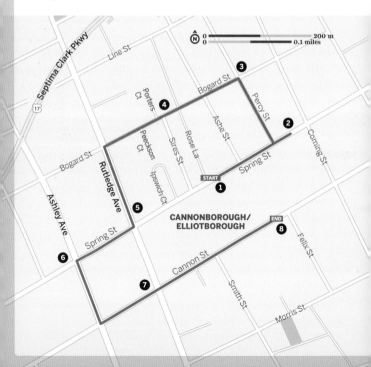

❶ Ice Bing

Kick things off at the new Taiwanese shaved-ice shop and teahouse **Ice Bing** (p74), which thrills residents with its foamy matcha lattes and rarely encountered *nai-gai* (tea with a milky, foamy sea-salt topping). Locals also adore the kind owners.

❷ Karpeles Manuscript Library

Exhibits at the **Karpeles Manuscript Library Museum** (p66) include Einstein's Theory of Relativity and Freud's manuscript on dreams. They rotate three times a year, which keeps the neighborhood residents stopping back in to see what's new.

❸ Elliotborough Mini Bar

Decked out in colored lights and funky art, tiny **Elliotborough Mini Bar** (☎843-577-0028; 18 Percy St; ⏱5-10pm Mon-Thu, to 11pm Fri & Sat, 3-8pm Sun) cheerfully serves beer and wine at prices locals love. The intimate venue also hosts regular live music sessions.

❹ George Gallery

The polar opposite of some of the schlocky galleries downtown, the decidedly non-touristy **George Gallery** (p66) features mostly abstract and non-objective work. The art rotates often, which keeps the regulars' interest piqued.

❺ Xiao Bao Biscuit

No matter how many times one pops into **Xiao Bao Biscuit** (p67) for a Japanese cabbage pancake, one will always be back for more. There's just nothing like a great craft cocktail with some spicy pan-Asian fare.

❻ Eclectic

At hyper-local **Eclectic** (p71), browse the vinyl collection and sip a latte in good company; it's a prime hangout spot for College of Charleston adjuncts and neighborhood creatives.

❼ Fuel

Round things out with a delicious mojito on the porch at **Fuel** (☎843-737-5959; www.fuelcharleston.com; 211 Rutledge Ave; ⏱11am-11pm), a classic Caribbean-themed neighborhood bar that attracts a cross section of students and young professionals.

❽ Sugar Bakeshop

The icing on the cupcake is **Sugar Bakeshop** (www.sugarbake.com; 59 1/2 Cannon St; cupcakes $3.25; ⏱10am-6pm Mon-Fri, 11am-5pm Sat), where in-the-know Charlestonians satisfy their sweet teeth, particularly on Thursday. That's Lady Baltimore day, and everybody loves this retro Southern specialty with dried fruit and white frosting.

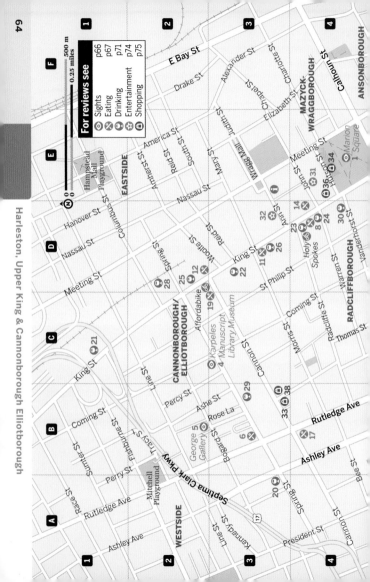

For reviews see
- Sights p66
- Eating p67
- Drinking p71
- Entertainment p74
- Shopping p75

500 m
0.25 miles

E Bay St

EASTSIDE

ANSONBOROUGH

MAZYCK-
WRAGGBOROUGH

Marion
Square

CANNONBOROUGH/
ELLIOTBOROUGH

RADCLIFFBOROUGH

Karpeles
Manuscript
Library Museum

George
Gallery

WESTSIDE

Septima Clark Pkwy

Mitchell
Playground

Hampstead
Mall
Playground

Rutledge Ave

Ashley Ave

Anson St
George St
Society St
Meeting St

Hasell St

Horlbeck Al

Meeting St

Gibbes 2
Museum
of Art

King St

Broad St

Kahal Kadosh
Beth Elohim

HISTORIC 37
DISTRICT

Market St

13

Princess St
Fulton St
Clifford St

Orange St

Gateway
Walk

Legare St

King St
35
15

Beaufain St

Archdale St

Queen St

West St

Magazine St

College of 3
Charleston

George St
Philip St
Glebe St

7

Wentworth St

Logan St

Short St

New St

Corning St

Franklin St

Broad St

Trapman St

Cromwell Al

Trumbo St

Pitt St

Urban
Nirvana
10

Smith St

Bull St

HARLESTON
VILLAGE

Colonial
Lake
Park

Colonial
Lake

Vanderhorst St
Pitt St

Rutledge Ave

Broad St

Smith St

Ashley Ave

Montague St

Wentworth St

Beaufain St

Calhoun St

Canon
Park

Halsey St

Gadsden St

Lockwood Dr

Ashley Ave

Barre St

Mill St

Halsey Blvd

Calhoun St

Medical
University
of South
Carolina

Alberta
Sottile
Long Lake

Lockwood Dr

16

Jonathan Lucas St

President St

Charleston
City Marina

Ashley River

Courtenay Dr

Sights

Marion Square   SQUARE

1 ⊙ MAP P64, E4

Charleston's most frequented park is 10 acres of green space in the middle of downtown, bordering on King, Calhoun, Meeting and Tobacco Sts. It's the home of the wildly popular Farmers Market (p75) and also houses several monuments, including a soaring statue of former Vice President John C Calhoun. (☏843-724-7327; www.nps.gov/nr/travel/charleston/mar.htm; 329 Meeting St; ⏱24hr)

Gibbes Museum of Art   GALLERY

2 ⊙ MAP P64, F7

Houses a decent collection of American and Southern works. The contemporary collection includes works by local artists, with Lowcountry life as a highlight. A 2016 renovation added a new museum store and cafe as well as 30% more gallery space. (☏843-722-2706; www.gibbesmuseum.org; 135 Meeting St; adult/child $15/6; ⏱10am-5pm Tue & Thu-Sat, to 8pm Wed, 1-5pm Sun)

College of Charleston   COLLEGE

3 ⊙ MAP P64, E5

Spread over a few city blocks at the center of Charleston's downtown, this university was founded in 1770 and is the oldest in the state. The campus is notable for its lush landscaping, which includes live oaks draped in Spanish moss, as well as its historic mansions and homes, some of which contain residence halls and Greek institutions. (☏843-805-5507; www.cofc.edu; 66 George St)

Karpeles Manuscript Library Museum   MUSEUM

4 ⊙ MAP P64, C3

An outpost of the world's largest private collection of important original manuscripts and documents, housed in a former Methodist church built in 1856. Exhibits rotate three times a year, making this a popular stop with locals. They include Einstein's Theory of Relativity, Freud's manuscript on dreams and Darwin's conclusion to his Theory of Evolution. (☏843-853-4651; www.rain.org/~karpeles; 68 Spring St; admission free; ⏱11am-4pm Tue-Sun)

George Gallery   ART STUDIO

5 ⊙ MAP P64, B2

A neighborhood favorite, this contemporary art gallery displays mostly abstract and non-objective work of artists from the East Coast with some connection to Charleston. There are no actual rules, though – just whatever the owner feels like. (☏843-579-7328; http://georgegalleryart.com; 50 Bogard St; ⏱10am-5pm Tue-Fri, 11am-5pm Sat)

Eating

Xiao Bao Biscuit

ASIAN $

6  MAP P64, B3

Housed in a former gas station, with exposed-brick walls and concrete floor – this casual but stylish eatery hits the hipster high marks. But the food? Now we're talking. The short but palate-kicking menu spotlights simple pan-Asian fare enhanced by local ingredients and spicy flavors. For something different and memorable, try the *okonomiyaki* – a Japanese cabbage pancake – with egg and bacon. (www.xiaobaobiscuit.com; 224 Rutledge Ave; lunch mains $12, dinner mains $12-16; ⏰11:30am-2pm & 5:30-10pm Mon-Sat)

Basic Kitchen

HEALTH FOOD $$

7  MAP P64, E6

With dishes like avo toast, fresh sesame kale and rainbow bowls (which come with sweet-potato noodles, veggies, herbs and Thai peanut sauce), this healthy and delicious little cafe feels like something you'd stumble across in Bali. The surfboard decor and yummy fresh fruit juices do nothing to dispel that impression; and clearly, vegetarians are well served here. (📞843-789-4568; https://basickitchen.com; 82 Wentworth St; breakfast & lunch mains $8-14, dinner mains $13-23; ⏰8-10:30am, 11am-3pm & 5:30-9pm Mon-Fri, 9am-3pm & 5:30-9pm Sat, 9am-3pm Sun; 🍴)

Marion Square

Gateway Walk

A loose, natural-feeling path, the **Gateway Walk** (Map p64) winds through several church grounds and overgrown graveyards between St John's Lutheran Church and St Philip's Church. The walk is particularly lovely during spring, when the wildflowers are in bloom.

Juanita Greenberg's Nacho Royale

MEXICAN $

 8 MAP P64, D4

Nachos are front and center at this tasty, affordable Mexican joint on King St, and locals go wild for it with good reason. The nacho royales arrive Mexican-pizza-style, with corn or flour chips and your choice of veggies, beans, steak, tofu, shrimp, pulled chicken and basically anything else you can dream of. Boring people can also get burritos or tacos. (📞843-723-6224; https://juanitagreenbergs.com; 439 King St; nachos $9-11; ⏱11am-2am)

Poogan's Porch

SOUTHERN US $$

9 MAP P64, F7

It's very Charlestonian to take brunch on the terrace of this cozy but elegant two-story Victorian, where the homemade buttermilk biscuits are out of control and the chicken and waffles are second to none. Boozy brunchers have their pick of mimosas, cocktails, craft beer and 1500 bottles of wine in the cellar. (📞843-577-2337; www.poogansporch.com; 72 Queen St; brunch mains $10-14, dinner mains $21-34; ⏱10:30am-2:30pm & 5-9:30pm Mon-Fri, 9am-2:30pm & 5-9:30pm Sat & Sun)

Circa 1886

SOUTHERN US $$$

 10 MAP P64, D7

In a renovated, elegant carriage house, this is Lowcountry fine dining at its most rewarding, with healthful, seasonal offerings that reflect the region's bounty and build on its traditions. Adventurous diners will appreciate the coffee-brined antelope, which comes with sorghum sweet-potato mousseline and shishito peppers. Everybody will lose it for the benne-crusted (sesame-crusted) duck breast with white peach grits.

There's also an extensive wine list, and the waitstaff are highly knowledgeable and gracious. (📞843-853-7828; www.circa1886.com; 149 Wentworth St; mains $34-40, tasting menu $90; ⏱5:30-10pm Mon-Sat)

Darling Oyster Bar

SEAFOOD $$

11 MAP P64, D3

Not all oysters are created equal in Charleston, but the Darling serves up the raw goodness. Its light, flavorful selections originate in places like Prince Edward Island and arrive at the table with a mild ginger mignonette. The Creole shrimp channels N'awlins and kills it, the lightly cured ceviche is highly refreshing, and the cocktails are crafty and delicious. (📞843-641-0821; http://thedarling. com; 513 King St; mains $10-27; ⏱4pm-late)

Ordinary
SEAFOOD $$

12 MAP P64, D2

Inside a cavernous 1927 bank building, this buzzy seafood hall and oyster bar feels like the best party in town. The menu is short, but the savory dishes are prepared with finesse – from the oyster sliders to the lobster rolls to the nightly fish dishes. (📞843-414-7060; www.eattheordinary.com; 544 King St; dishes $10-33; ⏱5-10:30pm Tue-Sun)

Le Farfalle
TUSCAN $$$

13 MAP P64, E6

Seafood charcuterie doesn't get better than the octopus carpaccio at Le Farfalle, a breath of fresh Tuscan air with a spacious, bright dining room and cheeky yet sophisticated waitstaff. The warm rosemary focaccia, housemade pastas and mains (ie roasted duck and sea bass) are all dreams on plates, and the extensive wine list makes for delightful pairings. (📞843-212-0920; http://lefarfalle charleston.com; 15 Beaufain St; pasta $17-26, mains $28-42; ⏱11:30am-2:30pm & 5:30-11pm Mon-Sat, 10:30am-2:30pm & 5:30-11pm Sun)

Halls Chophouse
STEAK $$$

14 MAP P64, D4

Hands down the best restaurant for getting all done up, squeezing in at the bar and ordering a sizable, rare cut of steak with several glasses of Napa Valley cabernet. (📞843-727-0090; https://hallschop house.com; 434 King St; steaks from $40; ⏱5-11pm Sun-Thu, to midnight Fri & Sat)

Leyla Fine Lebanese Cuisine
LEBANESE $$$

15 MAP P64, E5

A welcome respite from all the Lowcountry and fried food, this elegant Lebanese restaurant is a favorite with locals. You can't really go wrong, so you might as well do it all with a sampler of hummus,

---

Spa Day

On the grounds of the Wentworth Mansion, in gorgeously converted former stables, the elegant, relaxing **Urban Nirvana** (Map p64; 📞843-724-6555; www.urbannirvana.com; 141 Wentworth St; ⏱9am-7pm Mon-Sat, 11am-6pm Sun) spa is defined by brick and exposed wood beams. Complete with heated blankets and aromatic oils, the treatments are nothing short of transportive. The woman who does the facials (from $60) is a real pro.

tabouleh, baba ganoush, falafel, fried kibbe and lots of other goodness. There are plenty of good vegetarian options. (☎843-501-7500; http://leyla-charleston.com; 298 King St; mains $24-38; ⊙11:30am-9pm Tue-Thu & Sun, to 10pm Fri & Sat; 🖋)

Marina Variety Store

SOUTHERN US $

16 🍴 MAP P64, A7

A long-standing, down-home, greasy-spoon kinda place, with harbor views and Southern hospitality as warm as the buttermilk biscuits. Thumbs up to the grits, fried green tomatoes and crab cake Benedict. Put the gravy on everything. (☎843-723-6325; www.varietystorerestaurant.com; 17 Lockwood Dr; mains from $6; ⊙6:30am-4pm & 5-9pm Mon-Sat, 6:30am-3pm Sun)

Hominy Grill

SOUTHERN US $

17 🍴 MAP P64, B4

Slightly off the beaten path, this neighborhood cafe serves modern vegetarian-friendly Lowcountry cuisine in an old barbershop. The shaded patio is tops for brunch, and the 'nasty biscuit' is a crowd pleaser. (☎843-937-0930; www.hominygrill.com; 207 Rutledge Ave; breakfast $4.50-14, lunch & dinner mains $9-22; ⊙7:30am-3pm Mon-Fri, 9am-3pm Sat & Sun; 🖋)

Husk

SOUTHERN US $$$

18 🍴 MAP P64, F7

The creation of acclaimed chef Sean Brock, Husk is one of the

Xiao Bao Biscuit (p67)

South's most buzzed-about restaurants, which can be a disadvantage. How can the food possibly compete with the hype? (The fried chicken skins definitely don't.) Every ingredient is grown or raised in the South and the offerings change daily. The setting, in a two-story mansion, is elegant but unfussy. (📞843-577-2500; www. huskrestaurant.com; 76 Queen St; brunch & lunch $10-17, dinner $29-34; ⏰11:30am-2:30pm Mon-Sat, 5:30-10pm Sun-Thu, 5:30-11pm Fri & Sat, brunch 10am-2:30pm Sun)

Grocery AMERICAN $$$

19 🗺 MAP P64, C3

Set in an industrial-chic space adorned with mason jars of pickled everything, this is Charleston's farm-to-table champion, with a fiercely locavore and vegetarian-friendly approach, and cooking styles channeling both the South and the Mediterranean. Seasonal ingredients arrive fresh from nearby farmers, foragers and fishermen, and chef/owner Kevin Johnson combines them in innovative and deeply satisfying ways. (📞843-302-8825; www. thegrocerycharleston.com; 4 Cannon St; mains $28-30; ⏰5-10pm Tue-Sat, 10am-2:30pm & 5-10pm Sun; 🥗)

Drinking

Eclectic COFFEE

20 🗺 MAP P64, A3

Our favorite Charleston coffeehouse, this indigo-trimmed

Culinary Conundrums

So little time, so much deliciousness. Narrowing down where to eat on Upper King is the great Charleston challenge. The varied and eclectic eateries of Cannonborough Elliotborough don't make things easier.

Cannonborough Elliotborough establishment is gorgeous: the walls are lined with vinyl records for sale, and it has a perfect juxtaposition of hardwood flooring, exposed brick and silver-gilded ceilings, plus a gorgeous hand-hewed wooden workstation area reclaimed from an old South Dakota horse corral. Coffee, wine, beer and cafe grub mean you can stay here all day. (📞843-202-0666; www.eclectic cafeandvinyl.com; 132 Spring St; ⏰7am-7pm Mon & Wed, to 9pm Thu & Fri, 8am-9pm Sat, 9am-5pm Sun; 🛜)

High Wire Distilling DISTILLERY

21 🗺 MAP P64, C1

A bright downtown tasting room where you take shots of small-batch gin, whiskey, vodka and amaro, right in a row. Tasty cocktails are also available, and the 'bee's knees' (with botanical gin, lemon, honey and lavender) is a doozy.

Tours of the distillery run Tuesday through Saturday every hour (on the hour) from 11am to 6pm. Make a reservation. (📞843-755-4664;

http://highwiredistilling.squarespace.com; 652 King St; ⏰9am-6pm Tue-Fri, 11am-6pm Sat)

Prohibition

COCKTAIL BAR

22 🚍 MAP P64, D3

This delightful Jazz Age gastropub serves up excellent craft cocktails (from $10) that tend to pair well with the lip-smackin' Southern grub. Think a 'bacon maple old-fashioned' cocktail with some deviled eggs, or a mint julep with shrimp and grits. There's also a sweet dance floor, and free swing-dancing lessons are offered Wednesday and Sunday at 6:30pm. It's a total hoot. (☏843-793-2964; https://prohibitioncharleston.com; 547 King St; ⏰5pm-1am Mon-Thu, 5pm-2am Fri, 11am-2am Sat, 11am-1am Sun)

Closed for Business

PUB

23 🚍 MAP P64, D4

A 42-tap selection of local and national craft brews (from $4.25) and hipster-rustic decor gives this inviting 'draft emporium' a neighborhood vibe and just the right amount of edge. (☏843-853-8466; www.closed4business.com; 453 King St; ⏰11am-midnight Sun-Wed, to 2am Thu-Sat)

Proof

COCKTAIL BAR

24 🚍 MAP P64, D4

It may be snug in here, but the cocktails ($9 to $13) sure are first-class and their mixologist is some kind of visionary. Case in point: the 'knuckleball' has Old

Grand-Dad, a spicy cola reduction, orange bitters and pickled boiled peanuts. (☏843-793-1422; www.charlestonproof.com; 437 King St; ⏰4pm-2am Mon-Fri, 6pm-2am Sat & Sun)

Pour Taproom

CRAFT BEER

25 🚍 MAP P64, D2

A new brewpub with a cool concept: on-tap, self-serve craft beer, wine and cocktails, where you pour it yourself and pay by the ounce. It's downtown, on the 9th floor of the Historic District Hyatt. There are also appetizers and sandwiches. (☏843-779-0810; www.charleston.pourtaproom.com; 560 King St; ⏰4-11pm Mon-Thu, noon-1am Fri & Sat, noon-11pm Sun)

Charleston Distilling Co

DISTILLERY

26 🚍 MAP P64, D3

A farm-to-bottle, independently owned, small-batch distillery on King St. Grab a flight of spirits or a cocktail and take a tour ($5) of the distillery, a sleek space with inlaid brick and wood paneling. Do it fast, though. Word on the street is that the business may move to John's Island to expand their operations. (☏843-718-1446; www.charleston distilling.com; 501 King St; ⏰11am-7pm, closed Wed & Sun)

Bar at Husk

BAR

Adjacent to the restaurant Husk (see 18 🍽 Map p64, F7), this intimate brick-and-worn-wood spot recalls

Understanding Religion

The New World was mostly populated by colonies founded by certain religious sects. Charleston was not among them. The 'Holy City,' as it came to be known for its multitudes of churches, was instead a haven for religious tolerance, and today more than 400 houses of worship call Charleston home.

The Most Famous Churches

Part of being the 'Holy City' is that your skyline should be defined by its steeples and spires. That's why in Charleston the law dictates that no building can be higher than the tallest church steeple.

The oldest church in Charleston (that's still standing) is St Michael's Episcopal Church, which dates back to 1761 and has seen the likes of George Washington and Robert E Lee worship here. Its bells are a big deal, and have been announcing the time and various events, including earthquakes, hurricanes, fires and attacks on the city, for more than 250 years.

The second most prominent church, St Philip's, was erected in 1835, but its Anglican congregation is older than that of St Michael's. Many famous people are buried in the church cemetery, one end point of the Gateway Walk (p68) through several church grounds.

The French Huguenots

Some of the earliest religious refugees to take Charleston up on its invitation were the French Huguenots, who were part of a Protestant movement that was largely rejected in France. The English, however, were happy to receive the Huguenots, particularly because many of them were prosperous merchants and professionals.

Jewish Heritage

In the heart of Charleston, **Kahal Kadosh Beth Elohim** (Map p64; 📞843-723-1090; www.kkbe.org; 90 Hasell St; ⏰10am-4pm Sun-Fri) is the oldest continuously used synagogue in the country, and the birthplace of the American Reform Judaism movement.

a speakeasy, with classic cocktails ($10 to $15), sphere ice and passionate attention to detail. (📞843-577-2500; www.husk restaurant.com/about/bar; 76 Queen St; ⏰4pm-late)

Bin 152
WINE BAR

27 🍷 MAP P64, F7

From the same couple behind Chez Nous comes this elegant downtown wine bar (glasses from

$15). It's low-lit, chic and festooned in impressive, rotating art and antiques (all for sale). But the best reason to go is to pair the adventurous wine selections with imported cheese (from $10), freshly baked bread and other charcuterie bits. (☏ 843-577-7359; www.bin152.com; 152 King St; ⊘4pm-2am)

Alley
BOWLING

28 🎳 MAP P64, D2

Super-fun bar to play Skee-Ball, table hockey, bowling and Pop-A-Shot. They've also got arcade games and decent pub food. Wednesday is trivia night and Tuesday has $2 bowling lanes after 9pm. (☏843-818-4080; www.thealleycharleston.com; 131 Columbus St; per lane per hour Sun-Thu $35, Fri & Sat $45; ⊘4pm-2am Mon-Wed, 11am-2am Thu-Sun)

Ice Bing
TEAHOUSE

29 🍵 MAP P64, B3

Ice Bing is an adorable Taiwanese teahouse in Cannonborough Elliotborough specializing in shaved ice and hot beverages like matcha lattes, bubble tea and *nai-gai* (jasmine or black tea with a milky, foamy sea-salt topping. Pair them with food like tapioca balls, bento bowls and sushi. The people who work here couldn't be sweeter. (☏843-718-3967; https://icebingcafe.com; 93 Spring St; ⊘8:30am-6pm Mon & Tue, to 7pm Wed & Thu, to 8pm Fri, 11am-8pm Sat, 11am-4pm Sun; 🛜)

Kudu
COFFEE, CRAFT BEER

30 ☕ MAP P64, D4

Rock up at 6:45am and order an excellent espresso or craft booze – we're not judging – at this hipster cafe and beer bar located just off Marion Sq.

Beer-wise there are a total of 20 taps, including a featured cask-conditioned ale, while the coffee menu and execution would make any barista proud. Take either in the courtyard, complete with gurgling fountain. (www.kuducoffeeandcraftbeer.com; 4 Vanderhorst St; ⊘6:45am-9pm Mon-Fri, 7am-9pm Sat, 8am-8pm Sun)

Entertainment

Charleston Music Hall
LIVE PERFORMANCE

31 ⭐ MAP P64, E4

An intimate performance venue with great acoustics and not a bad seat in the house. Ideal for live music or theater. (☏843-853-2252; www.charlestonmusichall.com; 37 John St; ⊘box office 10am-3pm Mon-Fri)

Music Farm
CONCERT VENUE

32 ⭐ MAP P64, D3

A popular downtown concert venue, with local and national acts from every imaginable genre. The place isn't very big; in the summertime it often fills up and gets pretty sweaty. (☏843-577-6989; http://musicfarm.com; 32 Ann St; ⊘varies)

Shopping

Beads on Cannon JEWELRY

33 🔒 MAP P64, B3

A massive store, with two floors full of stones, Czech glass, wire, leather, chains, Swarovski crystal, tools and rhinestones. The store also offers jewelry-making classes. (📞843-723-5648; www.beadsoncannon.com; 87 Cannon St; ⏰11am-5pm)

Farmers Market MARKET

34 🔒 MAP P64, E4

Stop by this terrific farmers market on Saturdays for local produce, homemade food and drinks, art, music, boiled peanuts and more. (www.charlestonfarmersmarket.com; Marion Sq; ⏰8am-2pm Sat Apr-Nov)

Croghan's Jewel Box JEWELRY

35 🔒 MAP P64, E5

Long-standing, family-owned jewelry store, offering pricey but gorgeous antique pieces, estate finds, engagement rings and other one-of-a-kind gifts on Upper King. (📞843-723-3594; www.croghans jewelbox.com; 308 King St; ⏰10am-5:30pm Mon-Fri, to 5pm Sat)

Blue Bicycle Books BOOKS

36 🔒 MAP P64, E4

Excellent new-and-used store with a great selection on Southern history and culture. (📞843-722-2666; www.bluebicyclebooks.com; 420 King St; ⏰10am-7:30pm Mon-Sat, 1-6pm Sun)

Farmers Market

JERAMEY LENDE/SHUTTERSTOCK ©

Charleston Crafts Cooperative ARTS & CRAFTS

37 🔒 MAP P64, F6

A pricey, well-edited selection of contemporary South Carolina–made crafts, such as sweetgrass baskets, hand-dyed silks and wood carvings. (📞843-723-2938; www.charlestoncrafts.org; 161 Church St; ⏰10am-6pm)

Indigo & Cotton CLOTHING

38 🔒 MAP P64, B3

Stocks high-end and innovative brands of clothing, footwear and accessories: for instance, Raleigh Denim, a company that stitches its jeans on vintage sewing machines. (📞843-718-2980; https://indigoandcotton.com; 79 Cannon St; ⏰11am-6pm Mon-Fri, to 5pm Sat)

Explore ✦

Charleston County Sea Islands

A dozen islands within an hour's drive of Charleston make up the Charleston County Sea Islands. Around 10 miles southeast of Charleston on the Mt Pleasant side, Sullivan's Island and Isle of Palms beckon day-trippers for sand-lounging and reveling on blue-sky days. Around 4 miles in the other direction brings you to James Island, one of the most urban of Charleston's barrier sea islands. Further south, Folly Beach is good for a day of sun and sand. The other end of the island is popular with surfers.

Upscale rental homes, golf courses and the swanky Sanctuary resort mark Kiawah Island, southwest of Charleston, where you'll find lucky visitors cruising on their bikes along one of the most gorgeous beaches in the South. Nearby Edisto Island (ed-is-tow) is a home-spun family vacation spot without a single traffic light.

Getting There & Around

Charleston's barrier sea islands are all accessed via a series of byways and bridges from the city, though not always with a connection from one to another. You'll need to take the long way round if you want to go from Sullivan's Island to Kiawah or Edisto Islands, for example.

Charleston County Sea Islands Map on p82

Folly Beach (p84) AARON HYSLOP/SHUTTERSTOCK ©

Top Sight 📷
McLeod Plantation

Many of the plantations around Charleston once belonged to the city's very wealthiest denizens. McLeod is not among them. The upper-middle-class owners of this Sea Island cotton farm strived to keep pace, and the enslaved workers were pushed to their limits. This sight is among the best for understanding of the prolonged mistreatment of African Americans in the South.

◎ MAP P82, E3

📞 843-795-4386

www.ccprc.com/1447/
McLeod-Plantation-
Historic-Site

325 Country Club Dr,
James Island

adult/child $15/6

🕐 9am-4pm Tue-Sun

McLeod Home

This 19th-century Victorian-style plantation home isn't furnished or particularly grand. The ground floor contains what was once a formal parlor, a dining room and a small library with simple woodwork. A 1920s renovation reversed the orientation and the backdoor became the front entrance and a small porch was replaced by a new portico with columns. An indoor kitchen was also installed.

While the house isn't much to see, the story of its unique series of occupants is revelatory. They include the McLeod family, the Confederate army, the Union army, a federal agency that aimed to help ex-slaves transition to freedom, and the Charleston County Park & Recreation Commission.

Transition Row

A row of cramped, basic wooden cabins on the property was originally built to house slaves, and until 1960 the cabins offered no electricity or running water (only one house ever included indoor plumbing). After the war, the cabins became transitional housing for freed slaves, and a look inside gives visitors considerable insight into how generations of Gullah families lived.

After the McLeods regained control of the property, the cabins were rented out as family homes, often to the descendants of former slaves, until the last McLeod's death in 1990.

Places of Worship

Over the years, there were a couple of different structures that served as places of worship on the McLeod Plantation. In one of the old barns, a minister who was paid by Mr McLeod preached to African Americans about how they were to serve God by obediently performing their duties on the plantation.

The property also contains a former slave cabin that was converted into a worship house

★ Top Tips

o Bring tissues; even the tour guides here occasionally break down crying.

o Researcher Barbara Brundage occasionally gives highly informative and engaging tours; call ahead and time your visit for when she's working.

o Enrich your experience by downloading the Transition to Freedom app from Apple's App store, or borrow an Apple device from the welcome center.

o Arrive a bit before the formal tour to wander the grounds and read displays; you'll get more out of the guided tour.

✕ Take a Break

In a plaza near the plantation, Cory's Grilled Cheese (p88) offers comforting sandwiches loaded with cheese.

Occupants of the McLeod Plantation

The McLeod plantation home was built by slave labor just before the Civil War, and its first owner, William Wallace McLeod, also ordered a fence constructed around the house, which he referred to as 'the enclosure.' This was to separate his family space from the homes of the enslaved.

During the Civil War, the McLeod family (and all island residents) were forced to evacuate, and the plantation was occupied by Confederate soldiers. In 1865 the Union army took control of the island and made the McLeod plantation their headquarters, then turned it over to the Bureau for Refugees, Freedmen and Abandoned Lands, a government agency that helped transition four million ex-slaves to freedom. The home briefly served as a school for freed children and as a medical treatment facility, and parcels of the land were doled out to ex-slaves to build new lives.

In 1868 the political climate changed, the agency helping ex-slaves shuttered its doors and the McLeod family managed to claw back the property. For the next 100 years, the family maintained control over a work force of ex-slaves that lived and toiled in much the same conditions as they had before the war. Laws were passed that resembled the old slave code, punishments continued to be more severe than in a free-labor society, and the dream of land ownership receded into impossibility as payment for labor came in food rations and a portion of the harvest.

The last member of the McLeod family died in 1990 and left instructions in a will for the plantation to be preserved. Today it is managed by the Charleston County Park & Recreation Commission.

in the 1970s. From here, the Children of God Mission regaled James Island residents with gospel music via transistor radio.

Gullah Cemetery

Perhaps the most telling site on the plantation grounds is a wooded area that doubles as a Gullah cemetery, where more than 100 people are anonymously buried. The remains of children are contained in 42 of the graves, a testament to the brutal conditions on the plantation. Gullah people believed in an afterlife in which they rejoined their African ancestors.

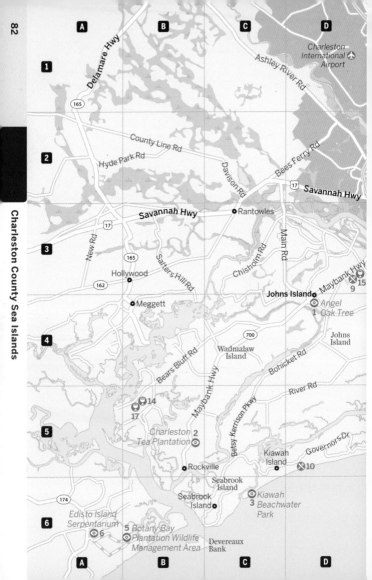

A **B** **C** **D**

1

Delamare Hwy

165

Charleston
International
Airport

Ashley River Rd

2

County Line Rd

Hyde Park Rd

Davison Rd

Bees Ferry Rd

17

Savannah Hwy

3

Savannah Hwy

Rantowles

17

165

New Rd

Salters Hill Rd

Chisholm Rd

Main Rd

Maybank Hwy

9 15

Hollywood

162

Johns Island

Angel
1 Oak Tree

Meggett

700

Johns
Island

4

Bears Bluff Rd

Wadmalaw
Island

Maybank Hwy

Bohicket Rd

River Rd

17 14

Betsy Kerrison Pkwy

Governors Dr

5

Charleston
Tea Plantation 2

Kiawah
Island

10

Rockville

Seabrook
Island

174

Edisto Island
Serpentarium

Seabrook
Island

Kiawah
3 Beachwater
Park

6

6

5 Botany Bay
Plantation Wildlife
Management Area

Devereaux
Bank

A **B** **C** **D**

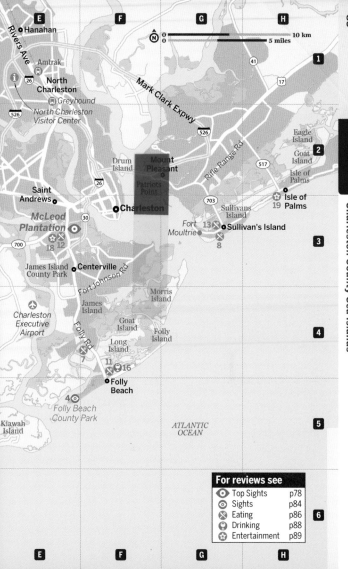

E Hanahan
Rivers Ave

F

G

H

0   10 km
0   5 miles

1

Amtrak
North
Charleston
Greyhound
North Charleston
Visitor Center

Mark Clark Expwy

41
17

Eagle
Island

2

Goat
Island
Isle of
Palms

Saint
Andrews

Drum
Island
Mount
Pleasant
Patriots
Point

Charleston

Rifle Range Rd

517

703

Sullivans
Island

Isle of
Palms ☆ 19

McLeod
Plantation ◉

30

☆ 18   12
James Island
County Park

700

Centerville

Fort Johnson Rd

Fort
Moultrie

13 ☒ ● Sullivan's Island

8 ☒

3

Charleston
Executive
Airport

James
Island

Morris
Island

Folly Rd

Goat
Island
Long
Island

Folly
Island

4

11
16

7

Folly
Beach

Kiawah
Island

4 ◉
Folly Beach
County Park

ATLANTIC
OCEAN

5

For reviews see
◉ Top Sights   p78
◉ Sights   p84
☒ Eating   p86
◐ Drinking   p88
☆ Entertainment   p89

6

E

F

G

H

Sights

Angel Oak Tree
HISTORIC SITE

1 MAP P82, D4

Some folks reckon this Southern live oak tree is 1500 years old (others says it's 400 to 500 years old). Whatever the case, it's one of the oldest living organisms east of the Mississippi, standing 66.5ft tall and measuring 28ft around. Its thick branches shoot off in all directions, in many cases twisting to the ground and back up again. There's no climbing allowed.

A small gift shop contains tree art and various books, and about 15 signs forbidding visitors from reading the books without purchasing them. (☏843-559-3496; www.angeloaktree.com; 3688 Angel Oak Rd, Johns Island; admission free; ⏰9am-5pm Mon-Sat, 1-5pm Sun, gift shop till 4:30)

Charleston Tea Plantation
PLANTATION

2 MAP P82, B5

There's only one large-scale, working tea plantation in the US, folks, and this is it. A trolley tour takes visitors around the property, offering plenty of information on its history, while a free tour of the production facility gives insight into the magic behind green, oolong and black tea. The gift shop has lots of goodies and souvenirs, including free, bottomless hot and cold tea. (☏843-559-0383; www.charlestonteaplantation.com; 6617 Maybank Hwy, Wadmalaw Island; trolley tour adult/child under 13yr $12/6; ⏰10am-4pm Mon-Sat, noon-4pm Sun)

Kiawah Beachwater Park
BEACH

3 MAP P82, C6

This idyllic stretch of sun-toasted sand at the southern end of Kiawah Island has been called one of the top 10 beaches in the USA and is the only publicly accessible beach on Kiawah. Take a bike – the compact sand is perfect for a ride along the 10-mile barrier island. (www.ccprc.com; 8 Beachwalker Dr, Kiawah Island; parking $5; ⏰9am-8pm May-Sep, shorter hours rest of year)

Folly Beach County Park
PARK

4 MAP P82, E5

At the far west end of Folly Beach, this scenic county park features a serene swimming beach and a pelican rookery. Public changing areas and beach-chair rentals are available. Lifeguards are on duty seasonally. (☏843-762-9960; www.ccprc.com; 1100 W Ashley Ave, Folly Island; parking $5-15; ⏰9am-8pm May-Aug, shorter hours rest of year)

Historic fort

Fort Moultrie (☏843-883-3123; www.nps.gov/fosu; 1214 Middle St, Sullivan's Island; adult/child $3/free; ⏰9am-5pm), at the mouth of Charleston Harbor, encapsulates the history of US coastal defense spanning nearly 200 years and four wars.

Botany Bay Plantation Wildlife Management Area

WILDLIFE RESERVE

5 MAP P82, B6

An avenue of regal live oaks flanks the entrance to this 4687-acre wildlife preserve, where a mix of pine forests, agricultural fields, coastal islands and two miles of undeveloped beach await. There's a 6.5-mile wildlife drive through the forest, which features plenty of birds and fox squirrels.

And the beach, which can only be accessed on foot, offers a peek at some coastline that looks similar to how it did when the original settlers arrived. In the 1800s the area was home to two successful Sea Island cotton plantations, Bleak Hall and Sea Cloud. (☏843-442-8140; Edisto Island; admission free; ☉sunrise-sunset Wed-Sun; 🐾)

Edisto Island Serpentarium

ZOO

6 MAP P82, A6

Around 50 years of reptile obsession by owners Ted and Heyward Clamp culminate in this serpentarium, which differs from most in that you can see snakes living in their natural habitats, separated from visitors by low-walled enclosures rather than glass. Alligators, lizards, turtles and crocodiles also live here. Think of it as a reptilian Disneyland. (☏843-869-1171; www.edistoserpentarium.com; 1374 Hwy 174, Edisto Island; adult/child $15/11; ☉10am-6pm Mon-Sat Jun-early Sep, hours vary Thu-Sat spring & fall)

Charleston County Sea Islands Sights

Angel Oak tree

DALE DUDLEY/SHUTTERSTOCK ©

Worth a Trip: Bulls Island

For a further-flung island adventure, nature enthusiasts will appreciate **Bulls Island** (☏843-881-4582; www.bullsislandferry.com; Awendaw; ferry ride $40), about an hour's drive north of Charleston. Its pristine shores can be reached via ferry (a 15-minute ride from the mainland), and captains often share their wealth of knowledge on the island's attractions, which include hiking trails, great shelling, numerous alligators and a 'boneyard' beach with spooky, bare trees poking up through the sand. It's wise to bring sunscreen, comfy shoes, a beach towel and some food. The boat stays at the island for a little over three hours, then heads back to the mainland.

If you've still got energy at this point, it's totally worth it to continue driving north to McClellanville, a quaint little fishing town with oak-lined streets and lovely Victorians. The superlative seafood joint **TW Graham & Co** (☏843-887-4342; http://twgrahamcoseafood.webs.com; 810 Pinckney St; mains $7-12; ⏰11am-2:30pm Tue-Sun & 5:30-9:30pm Thu-Sat) has expertly fried seafood and decadent key lime pie. Those who really like to make the most of their travels should consider a drive over a dirt road through the woods to the **St James Santee Parish Church** (Brick Church at Wambaw; Old Georgetown Rd, McClellanville), a little brick house of worship built in 1768 for the French Huguenots.

Another worthwhile attraction in the area is the **Center for Birds of Prey** (☏843-971-7474; www.thecenterforbirdsofprey.org; 4719 Hwy 17 N, Awendaw; tour & flight demonstration adult/child 6-12yr $18/12; ⏰10am-5pm Thu-Sat), where owls, hawks, falcons, kites, vultures and eagles are rehabilitated. Those that cannot be released stay within the 152-acre conservation area, and some birds do flying demonstrations.

Eating

Bowens Island Restaurant   SEAFOOD $

7 ⊗ MAP P82, F4

Down a long dirt road through Lowcountry marshland near Folly Beach, this unpainted wooden shack is one of the South's most venerable seafood dives – grab an oyster knife and start shucking!

A half/full tray runs $12/17. Cool beer and friendly locals give the place its soul. (www.bowensisland. biz; 1870 Bowens Island Rd, Folly Island; mains $8-18; ⏰5-9:30pm Tue-Sat)

Obstinate Daughter   AMERICAN $$

8 ⊗ MAP P82, G3

Sullivan's Island wasn't on the region's culinary map till this place showed up and made serious waves. The chef/owner, who also received high praise for Wild Olive, has demonstrated considerable range here, refocusing on light and playful plates of fresh veggies, pasta, seafood and unusual ingredients. Raw oysters are flown in from top locales, and vegetarians will leave exuberant.

The sun-drenched dining room is up on the 2nd floor, while a downstairs coffee shop and retail space offers strong coffee and lip-smacking gelato. (☏843-416-5020; www.theobstinatedaughter.com; 2063 Middle St, Sullivan's Island; pizza from $15, mains $10-27; ⏰11am-10pm Mon-Fri, 10am-10pm Sat & Sun; ✈)

Wild Olive ITALIAN $$

9 ✗ MAP P82, D3

This cozy Italian kitchen on Johns Island is whipping up some of the best homemade pastas and ambitious mains outside of Tuscany. The *carne crudo* is light and artful, and the lamb-sausage lasagna is a gooey delight that warmed us from the inside. Other favorites include charred octopus and ricotta gnocchi, and the homemade limoncello was a lovely touch.

The wine list is extensive and impressive. (☏843-737-4177; www.wildoliverestaurant.com; 2867 Maybank Hwy, Johns Island; pastas $13-22, mains $20-37; ⏰5:30-10pm Sun-Thu, to 11:30pm Fri & Sat, bar from 4pm; Ⓟ)

Jasmine Porch SOUTHERN US $$$

10 ✗ MAP P82, D5

Kiawah Island is a private island, mostly for fancy golfers and other well-off folks. But tell 'em at the gate you're headed to Jasmine Porch and, boom, you're in. The charming Southern kitchen is ensconced in the Sanctuary resort and its spacious dining room is defined by a sky-high ceiling, oak-plank flooring and elegant brick.

This is the place for she-crab soup, fried green tomatoes and anything from the sea, which you can also look out at through floor-to-ceiling windows. (☏843-768-6330; https://kiawahresort.com/dining/jasmine-porch; Kiawah Island; small plates $10-16, mains $26-36; ⏰6:30-11am, 11:30am-2pm & 5:30pm-late Mon-Sat, 6:30-10:15am, 11:45am-2pm & 5:30pm-late Sun)

Jack of Cups PUB FOOD $

11 ✗ MAP P82, F4

This local watering hole looks like your average neighborhood pub, with a sunny back patio, to boot. But the from-scratch menu, which

Freeze your bills off

The **Bill Murray Look-a-Like Polar Plunge** (Folly Beach) is a sub-zero swim that pays homage to Charleston's most distinguished resident each New Year's Day. Participants attempting to resemble Bill Murray in various roles, and everyone is encouraged to 'freeze your bills off.' Prizes are given to the best costumes.

changes daily, really sets it apart. The curries are excellent, and the mulligatawny soup – a red lentil concoction with Indian spices and apple puree on top – is rightfully famous. (📞843-633-0042; www. jackofcups.com; 34 Center St, Folly Beach; mains $9-12; ⏱kitchen noon-10pm Wed-Mon, bar open later)

Cory's Grilled Cheese SANDWICHES $

12 ⊗ MAP P82, E3

No hipster pretension here, just your average everyday strip-mall grilled-cheese joint with holes in the wall from weekend heavy-metal concert moshing. Cory's grilled-cheese sandwiches are gooey, buttery perfection (we dig the Lowcountry with pimento cheese, Muenster, avocado and bacon on sourdough), and there's beer too. (📞843-641-7377; www. corysgrilledcheese.com; 1739 Maybank Hwy, James Island; sandwiches $5.50-8.50; ⏱9am-3pm Mon, to 9pm Tue-Sat, to 5pm Sun)

Poe's Tavern PUB FOOD $

13 ⊗ MAP P82, G3

On a sunny day the front porch of Poe's on Sullivan's Island is the place to be. The tavern's namesake, master of the macabre Edgar Allan Poe, was once stationed at nearby Fort Moultrie. The burgers are good, and the Amontillado comes with guacamole, jalapeño jack, pico de gallo and chipotle sour cream. Quoth the raven: 'Gimme more.' (📞843-883-0083;

www.poestavern.com; 2210 Middle St, Sullivan's Island; mains $9-13; ⏱11am-midnight)

Drinking

Firefly Distillery DISTILLERY

14 MAP P82, B5

The world's first hand-crafted sweet-tea-flavored vodka came from this gem of a distillery, tucked into the forest on Wadmalaw Island. Sampling this classic, which is made with tea grown on the nearby Charleston Tea Plantation (p84), distilled four times and blended with sugarcane from Louisiana, is what brings most people to the door. Tastings are $6.

Once inside, though, guests sample a great many other libations, including flavored moonshines (the peach is insanely delicious), liqueurs that taste just like pies, and craft beer. Next door, Deep Water Vineyard, the only vineyard in the region, offers tastings as well, and on Saturdays there's also live music and food trucks. (📞843-557-1405; http:// fireflyspirits.com; 6775 Bears Bluff Rd, Wadmalaw Island; ⏱11am-5pm Tue-Sat)

Low Tide Brewing BREWERY

15 🍺 MAP P82, D3

A friendly neighborhood brewery with 12 taps spouting solid craft beers, including stouts, sours, ales and lagers. We like the Romance in the Dark, a dark sour with a hint of cherry flavor. A flight of four costs $7. (☏843-501-7570; http://lowtidebrewing.com; 2836 Maybank Hwy, Johns Island; ⊘3-10pm Mon-Thu, noon-midnight Fri & Sat, noon-10pm Sun)

Chico Feo
PUB

16 🍴 MAP P82, F4

A laid-back local favorite serving beer and wine, and also a range of tasty international dishes, from acai bowls to tacos to burritos to *bun cha* (a Vietnamese stew). (☏843-906-2710; www.chicofeos.com; 122 E Ashley Ave, Folly Beach; ⊘noon-2am Mon-Thu, 11am-2am Fri-Sun)

Deep Water Vineyard
WINERY

17 🍴 MAP P82, B5

OK, so muscadine wine isn't usually at the top of an oenophile's list. It is, however, a fine product of South Carolina, and at this here winery (the only one in the Charleston area, mind you), a few of them aren't that terrible. The owners bring in some grapes from California to make interesting blends with their own. Tastings are $7.

So although most of the wines still have that syrupy muscadine flavor, some kinda don't.Next door is Firefly Distillery, where the moonshine and liquors go down smooth as pie. (☏843-559-6867; www.deepwatervineyard.com; 6775 Bears Bluff Rd, Wadmalaw Island; ⊘10am-5pm Tue-Sat)

Nightlife

Folly Beach is the best (and edgiest) for nightlife, with a few bars in the island's center by the Tides Hotel. Sullivan's Island skews yuppie and has great people-watching. Isle of Palms has a good scene as well, particularly in the summer. There are a few good craft breweries on Johns Island.

Entertainment

Pour House
CONCERT VENUE

18 ⭐ MAP P82, E3

An intimate local music venue, with a very chill back patio. College kids and twenty-somethings dig it. (☏843-571-4343; http://charlestonpourhouse.com; 1977 Maybank Hwy, James Island; concerts from $12; ⊘4pm-2am Mon-Fri, to midnight Sat, 11am-2am Sun)

Windjammer
LIVE MUSIC

19 ⭐ MAP P82, H3

A long-standing beach bar with good live music Thursday through Saturday nights. Occasional karaoke, too. (☏843-886-8596; www.the-windjammer.com/wp; 1008 Ocean Blvd, Isle of Palms; tickets from $5; ⊘11am-1:30am)

Worth a Trip 👀
Fort Sumter National Monument

Fort Sumter National Monument, where the first shots of the Civil War were fired, certainly draws the crowds. Across the harbor on Sullivan's Island, Fort Moultrie and its richly layered history are also part of the monument. Together these fortifications illuminate the power struggles that plagued Charleston Harbor through four major wars and over 200 years.

Getting There

Take the **Fort Sumter Boat Tour** (Map p50, H4; www.fortsumtertours. com; adult/child 4-11yr $22/14) from Liberty Sq and Patriot's Point. This is the only way to get here.

The fort itself isn't physically imposing or visually impressive, but for a traveler with even a passing interest in American history, a trip to Sumter is requisite. The fort is named after Revolutionary War patriot Thomas Sumter, and its construction on an artificial island, in large part undertaken by enslaved laborers and craftspeople, began in 1829. Its 5ft-thick brick walls towered about 50ft over the water and supported several tiers of weaponry, though they were still unfinished in 1860 when Federal troops moved in.

The Fort Under Attack

On April 12, 1861, Confederate forces fired on the fort, and less than two days later the Union surrendered. The port of Charleston became a loophole in the blockade of the Atlantic coast, allowing the Confederacy to receive needed supplies and to continue exporting cotton. They held it for nearly four years, until General William T Sherman and his troops forced an evacuation in 1865. The fort was mostly unused until after WWII, when it became part of the National Monument.

Your Visit

Upon arrival, you'll disembark the ferry and gather around a national park ranger, who'll give an entertaining and efficient talk on the history of the site and its role in the Civil War. From there you'll have about an hour to wander the fort and its small museum. A map provided by the park can help you decide how to spend your time.

Fort Sumter Visitor Education Center

Getting to Fort Sumter requires hopping on a boat tour, and most of these leave from Liberty Sq, where the Fort Sumter Visitor Education Center is based. (The other jumping-off point is Patriot's Point in Mt Pleasant.) The visitor

---

⊙ MAP P26

☎ 843-883-3123; www.nps.gov/fosu

★ Top Tips

○ If you only have time for one fortification, visit Fort Moultrie. It's cheaper, more accessible and covers more historical ground.

○ Afternoon trips to Fort Sumter tend to be less crowded.

○ Book a combo ticket online for Fort Sumter and the USS *Yorktown* at Patriot's Point ($39).

✗ Take a Break

Buy snacks on the Fort Sumter ferry boat, as there are no restaurants around. Near Fort Moultrie on Sullivan's island, Obstinate Daughter (p86) is great for seafood, and Poe's Tavern (p88) is good for hamburgers. (FYI: Edgar Allan Poe was stationed at Fort Moultrie from 1827 to 1828.)

center offers exhibits on the roots of conflict that led to the Civil War, South Carolina's secession and the war's aftermath. It's a good primer before jumping on the boat, if you've got time, and is open daily from 8:30am to 5pm.

Fort Moultrie

Although it's not as famous as Fort Sumter, **Fort Moultrie** (☎ 843-883- 3123; www.nps.gov/fosu; 1214 Middle St, Sullivan's Island; adult/child $3/ free; ⏰ 9am-5pm) actually offers a deeper dive into the region's coastal defense systems, as its exhibits and structures span nearly 200 years. The fort standing today is the third version of Moultrie, and a very different structure than the first, which was composed of palmetto logs that held back the British in 1776. The site of that old fort is to the west of the present-day fort.

It is at the western tip of Sullivan's Island and to get there requires wheels

Outside the Walls

Other attractions outside the walls include the site of the second Fort Moultrie, which was destroyed by a hurricane in 1801. There's also a cannon walk, which showcases

Fort Moultrie

MEUNIERD/SHUTTERSTOCK ©

artillery pieces from the Civil War, and a burial site for Seminole leader Osceola, who died at the fort in 1838. Children and dogs will love to play on the fine white sands and climb the rocks on the adjacent beach.

Inside the Fort

Inside the fort, visitors can behold a WWII harbor command post, a couple of batteries designed in the early 1900s to protect the minefield, an exhibit of the modernization of weapons in 1870, and a display of the sweeping technological changes that happened during the Civil War. There's enough here to keep you busy for several hours, particularly if you're a history buff.

Fort Moultrie Visitor Center

Across the street from the fort, the visitor center has an information desk staffed by friendly park rangers, along with a theater, a museum and a bookstore.

Definitely check out the 22-minute documentary film

An Officer & a Gentleman

Pierre Beauregard, the Confederate general who commanded the attack on Fort Sumter, had been a student of Major Robert Anderson, the Union commander defending the fort, at West Point. Communications between the two men before the siege demonstrate the utmost respect.

on Fort Moultrie and the coastal defense system. It begins every half-hour in the theater.

The museum in here can be conquered in about 30 minutes, and includes artifacts and exhibits on the American Revolution, the Civil War, WWI and WWII (the fort evolved to meet the needs of each of these conflicts).

There is also some information on the slave trade at Sullivan's Island.

Explore ◈

Beaufort & Hilton Head Island

The southern half of the South Carolina coast is a tangle of islands cut off from the mainland by inlets and tidal marshes. Here, descendants of West African slaves known as the Gullah maintain small communities in the face of resort and golf-course development. The landscape ranges from tidy stretches of shimmery, oyster-gray sand to wild, moss-shrouded maritime forests.

On Port Royal Island, darling colonial Beaufort (byoo-furt) is the second-oldest city in South Carolina, and perhaps the nation's greatest educator on the turbulent post–Civil War period. The streets are lined with gorgeous antebellum homes, restored 18th-century mansions and twisting magnolias that drip with Spanish moss. Across Port Royal Sound, upmarket Hilton Head Island is South Carolina's largest barrier island and one of America's top golf spots. It was also the first eco-planned destination in the USA.

Getting There & Around

Most people use their own wheels in the Lowcountry. Those visiting Hilton Head usually fly into Savannah/ Hilton Head International Airport (p149) in Savannah, 40 miles west of the island. Beaufort is 71 miles southwest of Charleston International Airport (p149) and 46 miles northeast of Savannah/Hilton Head International Airport.

Beaufort & Hilton Head Island Map on p96

Harbour Town Lighthouse (p99) LARRY KNUPP/SHUTTERSTOCK ©

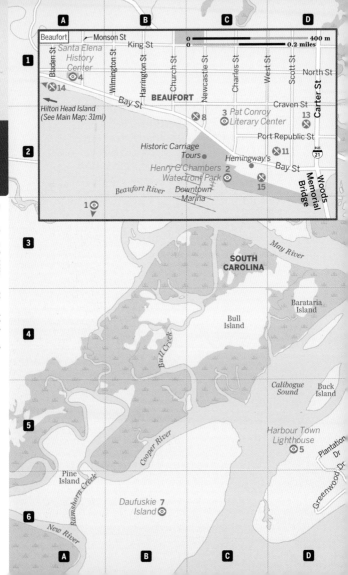

Beaufort

Monson St

King St

Santa Elena History Center ◎ 4

⊗ 14

Bladen St

Wilmington St

Harrington St

Church St

Newcastle St

Charles St

West St

Scott St

North St

Bay St

BEAUFORT

Craven St

Hilton Head Island (See Main Map; 31mi)

⊗ 8

3 Pat Conroy ◎ Literary Center

13 ⊗

Port Republic St

⊗ 11

BUS 21

Historic Carriage Tours ●

Hemingway's ●

Henry C Chambers Waterfront Park ◎

2

Bay St

Downtown Marina

⊗ 15

Woods Memorial Bridge

Beaufort River

1 ◎

SOUTH CAROLINA

May River

Barataria Island

Bull Island

Bull Creek

Calibogue Sound

Buck Island

Harbour Town Lighthouse ◎ 5

Plantation Dr

Cooper River

Pine Island

Daufuskie 7 Island ◎

Greenwood Dr

Ramshorn Creek

New River

0   400 m
0   0.2 miles

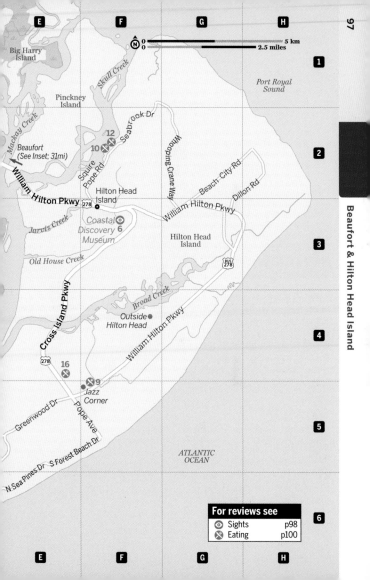

0 ————————— 5 km
0 ————————— 2.5 miles

Big Harry
Island

Port Royal
Sound

Pinckney
Island

Mackay Creek

Skull Creek

Seabrook Dr

Whooping Crane Way

Beaufort
(See Inset; 31mi)

William Hilton Pkwy

Squire
Pope Rd

12

10

Beach City Rd

Dillon Rd

Hilton Head
Island

278

William Hilton Pkwy

Jarvis Creek

Coastal
Discovery 6
Museum

Hilton Head
Island

Old House Creek

BUS
278

Cross Island Pkwy

Broad Creek

Outside
Hilton Head

William Hilton Pkwy

278

16

9

Jazz
Corner

Greenwood Dr

Pope Ave

ATLANTIC
OCEAN

N Sea Pines Dr

S Forest Beach Dr

For reviews see	
◎ Sights	p98
⊗ Eating	p100

6

Sights

Sandbar   NATURAL FEATURE

1 ◉ MAP P96, A3

At low tide on a warm day, Beaufort's sandbar is the place to drink and be drunk. It's only about a mile south of the Henry C Chambers Waterfront Park, and people show up in all manner of watercraft, including boats, kayaks and paddle boards. They bring coolers with enough booze to last long after the tide goes out, and on some days there are even concerts performed on a floating stage. (Beaufort River)

Henry C Chambers Waterfront Park   PARK

2 ◉ MAP P96, C2

Overlooking the bay, this iconic downtown anchor is flanked by dining options, shops and art galleries. Many of Beaufort's festivals and events are held here, and it's a really beautiful place to watch the sun dip behind the marina. (☎843-525-7011; Bay St)

Pat Conroy Literary Center   ARTS CENTER

3 ◉ MAP P96, C2

Until his death in 2016, South Carolina's literary great Pat Conroy called Beaufort home. The city inspired some of his most famous works, including *The Great Santini* and *The Prince of Tides*, and this newly established literary center offers exhibits on his life and work, including his writing desk and chair, and a handwritten prologue to *The Prince of Tides*.

The center also hosts events including the **Pat Conroy Literary Festival** (http://patconroyliterary festival.org; 308 Charles St; day pass from $73.50; ◷Oct) and readings by acclaimed authors. (☎843-379-7025; http://patconroyliterarycenter.org; 308 Charles St; ◷noon-4pm Thu-Sun)

Santa Elena History Center   MUSEUM

4 ◉ MAP P96, A1

Tucked into an old federal courthouse, this history museum tells the largely unfamiliar story of the earliest Europeans to settle in North America, and we're not talking about Jamestown.

Back in 1562 the French landed on present day Parris Island and dubbed it Charlesfort. They abandoned the site, but in 1566 the Spanish moved in and renamed it Santa Elena. This museum describes the early rivalry between these nations, and how the colonialists lived.

There's a short film to orient you before visiting the exhibits. Kids will enjoy the hands-on archaeological 'dig' for artifacts on the 1st floor. (☎843-379-1550; https://santa-elena.org; 1501 Bay St; $10; ◷10am-4pm Tue-Sat; ♿)

Harbour Town Lighthouse

LIGHTHOUSE, MUSEUM

5 ⊙ MAP P96, D5

Hilton Head's lighthouse, with the only female lighthouse keeper in North America, was built in 1970 and is prettily perched at the Harbour Town marina on the island's southern end, tucked away on Sea Pines Plantation. The 114 steps to the top are a museum, filled with Civil War artifacts, island history and regional lighthouse history, which certainly makes climbing them more interesting than otherwise. In addition to the admission, you'll pay a $6 day-pass fee for Sea Pines.

The entryway downstairs doubles as a maritime gift gallery, with nautical items and South Carolina books and memorabilia, and there's also a gift shop at the top. (www.harbourtownlighthouse. com; 149 Lighthouse Rd; adult/child $4.25/free; ⊙10am-sunset)

Coastal Discovery Museum

MUSEUM

6 ⊙ MAP P96, F3

A Smithsonian Affiliate, this Hilton Head museum is well worth a trip for its exhibits highlighting the island's rich Gullah history, natural wonders and other coastal treasures. A trail system on the 62-acre property winds past ancient oak trees, lush gardens and historic buildings. The museum suggests a donation of $5. (📞843-689-6767; www.coastaldiscovery.org; 70 Honey

Henry C Chambers Waterfront Park

Horn Dr; admission free; ⏰9am-4:30pm Mon-Sat, 11am-3pm Sun)

Daufuskie Island ISLAND

7 ◉ MAP P96, B6

For those looking for an escape just a touch less discovered than Hilton Head, this idyllic island offers a sublime day trip and a window into the Lowcountry's slower-paced past. The attractions of the island – a historical trail, a few restaurants, a couple of golf clubs, some art galleries, a winery and a rum distillery – are best visited via golf cart, the primary mode of transport on the island. Its shores are only accessible by boat.

For information about the ferry and water taxi, visit www.daufuskie islandferry.com. (www.hiltonhead island.org/daufuskie-island)

Food Scene

Beaufort has a smaller culinary scene than Charleston, but it isn't short on Lowcountry scrumptiousness or fresh seafood. A handful of good restaurants offer outdoor dining with views of the river, and the elegant Ribaut Social Club leads the pack.

Meanwhile, Hilton Head is known for its fresh Lowcountry seafood and an overall resistance to chain restaurants. The island thrives on locally owned, independently operated restaurants specializing in fresh-off-the-boat fish, shrimp, oysters and crab.

Eating

Ribaut Social Club AMERICAN $$

8 🍴 MAP P96, C2

A refined yet homey Lowcountry restaurant, set in the refurbished mansion **Anchorage 1770** (📞877-951-1770; https://anchorage1770. com; 1103 Bay St; r $235-375; ❄🛜) that once belonged to Admiral Beardslee (and named after his boisterous gentlemen's club).

The executive chef brings a personal touch to regional, seasonal dishes, and excels with seared sea scallops with Carolina gold rice and a tender duck breast in a pomegranate bourbon glaze.

Grab a pre-dinner drink in the parlor or on the 4th-floor terrace overlooking the Port Royal Sound, and don't miss the fabulous Sunday brunch.

Reservations are a great idea. (📞877-951-1770; https://anchorage 1770.com/dining.aspx; 1103 Bay St; mains $20-32; ⏰5-7:30pm Wed-Sat, 11am-2pm Sun)

Java Burrito MEXICAN $

9 🍴 MAP P96, F5

Like a sustainably tricked-out Chipotle, this family-owned, farm-to-table burrito Eden is impossible not to love, which is why in-the-know Hilton Head islanders are addicted to it. Choose your method (burrito, bowl, taco etc), choose your protein (chicken, steak, veggies, eggs,

Worth a Trip: St Helena, Parris and Hunting Islands

Within day-tripping distance from Beaufort, a cluster of marshy, rural islands offers an enticing amalgam of history, culture and nature, with a splash of Marine Corps action and some super-tasty shrimp burgers to boot.

Across the bridge to the east, **St Helena Island** is the heart of Gullah country, where the descendants of slaves have meticulously preserved their language and culture, and where two Reconstruction Era National Monuments were established by President Obama in 2017. For a deeper appreciation of all things Gullah, there's the long-standing **Gullah-N-Geechie Mahn Tours** (☑843-838-7516; www. gullahngeechietours.net; 16 Penn Center Circle W; per person from $32, minimum 2 people; ☺tours 9am, 11:30am, 1:45pm Mon-Sat).

Farther east, on **Hunting Island**, you'll find **Hunting Island State Park** (☑843-838-2011; www.southcarolinaparks.com/huntingisland; 2555 Sea Island Pkwy; adult/child 6-15yr $5/3; ☺park 6am-6pm, to 9pm Mar-Sep, visitor center 9am-5pm Mon-Fri, 11am-5pm Sat & Sun, nature center 9am-5pm Tue-Sat, daily Jun-Aug) – one of the state's most breathtaking coastal parks – and perhaps a shark tooth.

To the south, **Parris Island** features a Marine Corps training ground and **museum** (☑843-228-2951; www.parrisislandmuseum.com; 111 Panama St; admission free; ☺10am-4:30pm), and an archaeological site where the country's first European settlers landed.

And for kayak and stand up paddling (SUP) enthusiasts, tour company **Higher Ground** (☑843-379-4327; https://higherground outfitters.com; 95 Factory Creek Ct, Lady's Island; tours per person from $50, rental kayak or SUP half/full day $40/60; ☺10am-6pm Mon-Sat, 1-4pm Sun) has rental gear and trips out of Sea Island. As if all that isn't enough, the sweeping views from the bridges connecting these lowland isles are beyond postcard-pretty.

Should you get hungry, head for one of the roadside seafood places or Gullah restaurants (both are easy to come by on St Helena and Lady's Islands).

If you're headed to Hunting Island State Park, grab snacks and coffee at **Carolina Cider Company & Superior Coffee** (www.carolina ciderco.com; 507 Sea Island Pkwy, St Helena Island; ☺8am-6pm Mon-Sat, from 8:30am Sun, open longer hours in summer) or a famous shrimp burger at **Shrimp Shack** (☑843-838-2962; 1929 Sea Island Pkwy; mains from $3, shrimp burgers $8; ☺11am-2pm Mon-Sat).

Activities & Tours

Golf, bicycling and dolphin-watching are the prime activities on Hilton Head, and **Outside Hilton Head** (Map p96, F4; ☎800-686-6996; www.outsidehiltonhead.com; 1 Shelter Cove Lane; ☺8am-6pm summer, shorter hours rest of year) is the big water sports outfitter. Beaufort's got plenty of water sports, too, along with a plethora of tours.

Historic carriage tours (☎843-524-2900, 843-476-7789; 1002 Bay St; tour $23; ☺hours vary) are a great way to get acquainted with Beaufort's history. **Pat Conroy's Beaufort Tour** (☎843-838-2746; www.beauforttoursllc.com; adult/child 4-12yr $30/15; ☺2pm Thu-Sun) is highly recommended for fans of the author. Daredevils will enjoy **Vintage Biplane Tours** (☎904-910-6369; www.beaufortbiplanetours. com; 30-min flight $200; ☺11am-6pm).

local fish etc), choose your fixings (rice, beans, queso etc), then die happy.

From the Mexican dishes to the breakfast sandwiches to the parfait, everything is antibiotic- and hormone-free, locally and sustainably sourced, and tasty as hell. But that's not all! It doubles as an excellent coffee bar and has beer, wine, great peach margaritas and even champagne! (☎843-842-5282; www.javaburritoco.com; 1000 William Hilton Pkwy; mains $7-14; ☺7:30am-9pm Mon-Sat; 🛜)

Hudson's

SEAFOOD $$

10 ✖ MAP P96, F2

Hilton Head's go-to seafood shack is a doozy, with a wonderful dock-side deck on the water that brims with revelry (old-time islanders stick to the cozy indoor bar), all of which is centered on the bounties of the sea. Anything with shrimp,

(seasonal) soft-shell crab or fresh oysters (they cultivate and harvest their own seasonally) will woo you.

If it's not from these waters, it's not plated. And, incidentally, they might have the South's best hush puppies. (☎843-681-2772; www. hudsonsonthedocks.com; 1 Hudson Rd; lunch $9-24, dinner $14-34; ☺11am-3pm & 5-9pm; 🛜)

Old Bull Tavern

GASTROPUB $$

11 ✖ MAP P96, D2

The Old Bull Tavern offers some of the tastiest food and cocktails in Beaufort, with a wood-fired pizza oven and low-lit, worldly aesthetic to boot. The menu changes daily but always features playful American and European comfort dishes, prepared with fresh seasonal ingredients, often with a clever twist. Start with the wasabi deviled eggs and prosciutto, and continue with the braised lamb shank.

Wash it all down with a bourbon flight or a Yemassee cooler (rum, Aperol, lemon juice, blackberry shrub, orange bitters and soda). (📞843-379-2855; http://oldbulltavern.com; 205 West St; mains $13-18; ⏱5-9:30pm Tue-Thu, to 10pm Fri & Sat)

Skull Creek Dockside Restaurant
SEAFOOD $$

12 🍴 MAP P96, F2

Set in a renovated old river house, the latest addition to Hilton Head's dining scene raises the (already high) bar for seafood with its mouthwatering amalgam of American, Italian and Southern dishes. Think heaping plates of meat-heavy crab cakes, scallops seared in citrus butter and colossal stuffed shrimp, paired with sides like pimento-cheese grits and creamy collard greens.

The dining room is elegantly adorned in reclaimed wood with natural accents, and offers giant windows overlooking a newly refurbished dock. But dramatic warm-weather sunsets simply must be enjoyed from the covered patio or the outdoor bar. The wine list is excellent. (📞843-785-3625; www.docksidehhi.com; 2 Hudson Rd; mains $15-29; ⏱11am-10pm Mon-Thu, to 11pm Fri & Sat, 10am-10pm Sun)

Lowcountry Produce
SOUTHERN US $

13 🍴 MAP P96, D2

A fantastic Beaufort cafe and market for picnic rations such as pies, housemade relishes, local cheeses

Santa Elena History Center (p98)

JEFFREY GREENBERG/UIG VIA GETTY IMAGES ©

and all kinds of Lowcountry-spun awesomeness (including a bizarre but wildly popular cream-cheese lasagna). Or eat in and indulge in an Oooey Gooey, a grilled pimento-cheese sandwich with bacon and garlic-pepper jelly (one hot mess!), or a tasty crab-cake sandwich with brussels-sprouts slaw.

It's a madhouse here on weekends, for good reason. And the Bloody Marys are fabulous. (☎843-322-1900; www.lowcountry produce.com; 302 Carteret St;

Why Is Beaufort So Well Preserved?

In November 1861, Union forces prevailed in the Battle of Port Royal, laying siege to Confederate forts on Hilton Head Island and St Helena Island. When slave owners in Beaufort caught wind of this, they all skipped town in what a newspaper columnist famously dubbed Beaufort's 'Great Skedaddle.'

As tour guides tell it, white people left so fast that Union soldiers found half-eaten suppers on the tables. There was fear of a revolt, because back then Beaufort's population was 85% enslaved people. These newly freed African Americans were left behind to tend to the homes, all of which remain standing today. For this reason, Beaufort is an exceptional place to visit not only to view magnificent antebellum homes, but also to learn about the Reconstruction Era and the culture of the Gullah people, who are descendants of the ex-slaves.

After the war, Beaufort's infrastructure was largely converted into hospitals where soldiers and former slaves got medical care. Over on St Helena Island, Penn School was established to educate ex-slaves and provide social services and employment assistance. Darrah Hall, the oldest standing structure on the school grounds, is one of four sites that in 2017 was named a Reconstruction Era National Monument by President Obama. Others include the Brick Church, where classes were held, the Old Beaufort Fire House, a social and economic hub of the time, and Camp Saxton in Port Royal, where 5000 African Americans (many of whom were ex-slaves) were recruited to join the Union army.

Notable figures with connections to Beaufort include Harriet Tubman, conductor of the Underground Railroad, who worked here to liberate slaves and recruit them into the army. On carriage tours, visitors also pass the former home of Robert Smalls, an ex-slave who commandeered a Confederate ship, turned it over to the Union and became the period's most inspiring African American politician.

breakfast $9-15, sandwiches $10-18;
⏰8am-3pm; 📶)

Sgt White's   SOUTHERN US, BARBECUE $

14 🍴 MAP P96, A1

A retired Beaufort marine sergeant
serves up classic meat and three-
sides platters. At the counter,
order your juicy BBQ ribs, pork,
fish or shrimp dish, then choose
three sides, which can include
collards, okra stew and cornbread.
(📞843-522-2029; 1908 Boundary St;
meat & 3-sides platter $9; ⏰11am-
3pm Mon-Fri)

Plums   SOUTHERN US $

15 🍴 MAP P96, C2

A solid waterfront bistro in Beaufort serving creative Lowcountry
cuisine whipped up with local,
seasonal ingredients. Great sandwiches, salads and seafood, and
the shrimp-and-crab dip served
with warm pretzel-y bread is a
mouth's dream. (📞843-525-1946;
http://plumsrestaurant.com; 904 Bay
St; mains $10-15; ⏰11am-9pm)

Red Fish   SEAFOOD $$$

16 🍴 MAP P96, E4

Equal parts bottle shop, art gallery and intimate seafooder, Red
Fish hosts power-lunch cronies
by day and Hilton Head islander
foodies by night, both of whom

Drinking & Nightlife

Beaufort is called a 'two-liver
town,' meaning you'll need two
livers to do this place right.

The **Sandbar** (p98) is the
drinking spot of choice on
warm days, and **Hemingway's**
(📞843-521-4480; www.heming
ways.org; 920 Bay St; ⏰10am-
2am; 📶) is a hub regardless of
the weather. Locals you have
just met may invite you along:
just go.

On Hilton Head Island, most
of the independent nightlife is
concentrated on the south end
in an area known as the 'Bar-
muda Triangle.' **Jazz Corner**
(Map p96, F5; 📞843-842-8620;
www.thejazzcorner.com; 1000
William Hilton Pkwy; ⏰6-11pm) is
also a great spot for live music
and a martini.

come for hook-to-table seafood
(a co-owner's husband does
the fishing himself), paired with
excellent Californian and Oregon-
ian wines. Start with the baked
pimento-cheese appetizer, then
go for whatever's freshest, which
is often prepped with Asian and
Latin touches. (📞843-686-3388;
www.redfishofhiltonhead.com; 8 Archer
Rd; mains $24-39; ⏰11:30am-2pm &
5-9pm Mon-Sat; 📶)

Explore

Historic District & Forsyth Park

Fringed by Forsyth Park to its south, Savannah's Historic District – the largest National Historic Landmark District in the country – is home to 22 gorgeous squares that serve as a backdrop for exquisite 18th- and 19th-century homes, fascinating museums and monuments, and world-class restaurants, all enveloped by a dazzling canopy of Spanish-moss-laden live oak trees.

The sights of Savannah's Historic District are among the best in the country. Monuments, museums and grand homes will keep you wandering in wonder. The district is arranged in a grid, making it easy to walk from one end to the other, with Forsyth Park at the southern edge near the Victorian District, and River St to the far north. President St is the eastern boundary and Martin Luther King Jr Blvd is the western, where you'll find the visitor center.

Getting There & Around

The **JMR Transit Center** (610 W Oglethorpe Ave) just west of the Historic District is the city's local transport hub. You can catch the free 'dot' line for rides all around the area and to Forsyth Park. Taxis, pedicabs and bikes are also great ways to get around if you're staying close by.

Historic District & Forsyth Park Map on p112

Cathedral of St John the Baptist (p115) F11PHOTO/SHUTTERSTOCK ©

Top Sight 📷
Forsyth Park

Beloved of locals and visitors alike, Forsyth Park is abuzz with events and activities year-round. The sprawling green lawns, historic monuments and majestic fountain form the heart and soul of downtown Savannah's outdoor life – it's the place to come to be active, lay in the sun and have a picnic, or simply stroll around the paths and take in all its splendor.

🎯 MAP P112, C8

admission free

Inspired Design

Developed in the 1840s on 10 acres of land donated to the city by Savannah scholar-diplomat William Hodgson, Forsyth Park was part of Oglethorpe's original vision for the city and was expanded after Georgia governor John Forsyth donated an additional 20 acres that tripled the size of the park. In conceiving Forsyth's layout, Bavarian landscape designer William Bischoff took cues from the French. He was inspired by urban-renewal efforts taking place in Paris that featured neighborhoods radiating out from a central green space. In 1858 a fountain was installed and over the years, monuments to commemorate historic events in Savannah have been added, as well as a Garden of Fragrance for the blind, an outdoor amphitheater, a playground and tennis courts.

The Famous Founders

Forsyth's central fountain is the park's crown jewel and has become a distinctive icon of Savannah – but it's not quite as unique as people think.

When the fountain was decided upon in 1858, city council appointed a committee to choose a design...from a catalog. The design, simply known as 'No 5,' was one of a few elaborate options featured in a catalog of ornamental ironwork by Janes, Beebe & Company of New York. Modeled after a fountain designed by Michel Joseph Napoleon Lienard and cast by the JPV Andre Iron Foundry in Paris, its inspiration was sourced during the Great Exhibition of 1851 at the Crystal Palace in London's Hyde Park after a Janes, Beebe & Company representative was sent to research the manufacturing of garden ornaments.

One thing sets Forsyth's fountain apart, though: every St Patrick's Day, its waters are ceremoniously dyed green.

★ **Top Tips**

○ On Saturdays, check out the farmers market on the south end of the park.

○ Pick a patch of grass on the north side of the park near the fountain for more shade and a bit of an intimate feel.

○ Enjoy the park by day or night; just don't linger past midnight.

✕ **Take a Break**

The Sentient Bean (p133) is across the street from the park's south entrance on Park Ave – it has great coffee and tasty, healthy food.

Walking Tour 🥾

Savannah's Squares

One of the great joys of visiting Savannah is simply walking around the historic district amid some of the most beautiful residential architecture in the country. The city's original layout is an inspiring bit of urban planning: four open squares, each one ensconced within four residential and four civic blocks, a pattern that has repeated itself as Savannah has grown.

Walk Facts

Start: Forsyth Park

End: Johnson Sq

Length: 1¾ miles, two hours

❶ Forsyth Park

Begin this leisurely stroll at the south entrance of **Forsyth Park** (p108) at Bull St and Park Ave. Head north along the main thoroughfare and arrive at the iconic fountain for an obligatory photo op.

❷ Monterey Square

Stay north on Bull St toward the intersection of Wayne St, where a tall monument topped with a statue of General Casimir Pulaski greets you in **Monterey Sq**, one of Savannah's most picturesque.

❸ Mercer-Williams House

The **Mercer-Williams House** (p114), setting of the novel and film *Midnight in the Garden of Good and Evil*, faces its west side – pop in to hear the harrowing history of what went down inside Savannah's most famous haunted house.

❹ Chippewa Square

Chippewa Sq sits smack in the middle of the Historic District, with a bronze statue of Savannah founder James Oglethorpe overseeing all the action from the center.

❺ Wright Square

Keep truckin' north on Bull St, past Oglethorpe Ave, to York St and arrive at **Wright Sq**. This was the second square constructed in Savannah and is the burial site of Tomochichi, the Yamacraw tribe leader who befriended Oglethorpe and helped him establish the colony.

❻ Telfair Square

Head west on York St for two blocks to **Telfair Sq**. You won't find any monuments with a contentious backstory in this square, but you will find creative inspiration all around it – both the **Telfair Academy** (p114) and the **Jepson Center for the Arts** (p114) sit on Barnard St.

❼ Ellis Square

Continue north on Barnard St and cross over Broughton St, downtown's main commercial drag, toward Congress St to arrive at **Ellis Sq**. It was a center for commerce from the 1730s through the 1950s, and in the 1850s it housed a slave market.

❽ Johnson Sq

Head back east down St Julian St toward Bull St and end the journey at **Johnson Sq**, Savannah's first and largest square.

✕ Take a Break

Cool off at **Leopold's Ice Cream** (p118), the classic American dessert parlor where tutti-frutti was invented.

Savannah River

Savannah River

E River St
E Factors Walk
City Hall Landing
Riverwalk
W River St
Savannah Smiles
Dueling Pianos

Emmet Park

E Bay St

10 ✕
15 ✕

E Bryan St
Reynolds Sq

E Congress La
26 ⓘ
Footprints of Savannah

Leopold's Ice Cream

Warren Sq

Savannah Bike Tours

E Broughton St
E Broughton La
E State St
E President St
E York St
E York La

Oglethorpe Sq

Columbia Sq

E Oglethorpe Ave

Abercorn St

Lincoln St

Drayton St

Bull St

Johnson Sq

Wright Sq

28 ⓘ
14 ✕
9 ✕

Whitaker St

American Prohibition Museum
City Market
Ellis Sq
Jinx

24 ⓘ
22 ✕
13 ✕
W River St
W Bay St
W Bryan St
Franklin Sq
W Congress St

W Congress La
W Broughton St
W Broughton La
18 ⓘ
W State St

Telfair Academy
Telfair Sq

Jepson Center for the Arts

Barnard St

Jefferson St

Montgomery St

W York St

Chippewa Sq

Hull St
W McDonough St
W Perry St
W Perry La

Orleans Sq

W Oglethorpe La

Barnard St

Williamson St
W Bay St

Ann St

17 ✕
16 ✕

Martin Luther King Jr Blvd

W Oglethorpe Ave

Savannah Civic Center

23 ⓘ

Fahm St
Zubley St

Greyhound Bus Station

St Gaul St

W Turner Blvd

SCAD Museum of Art
5

Amtrak (3mi)

Savannah Visitors Center
1

Louisville Rd
W Harris St

Historic District & Forsyth Park

Colonial Park Cemetery

HISTORIC DISTRICT

Hull St
Price St
Habersham St

W Charlton St

W Liberty St
W Liberty La
W Harris St
W Charlton St
W Charlton La
Barnard St
W Jones St
W Taylor St
Jefferson St
Tattnall St
W Gordon St
W Gordon La
W Huntingdon St
W Hall St
W Gwinnett St

Montgomery St

Martin Luther King Jr Blvd

Montgomery St

Howard St
Barnard St
Whitaker St

Pulaski Sq

Chatham Sq

Forsyth Park

Bull St
Drayton St

27 🛍
19 🛍
Sorrel Weed House 3 ⊙
20 🛍
Madison Sq
25 🛍

Mercer-Williams House 1 ⊙
Monterey Sq

Drayton St
E Hall St

Cathedral of St John the Baptist 8 ⊙

Lafayette Sq

Flannery O'Connor Childhood Home 4 ⊙

Calhoun Sq

E Liberty St
E Harris St
E Charlton St
E Charlton La
E Jones St
E Jones La
Lincoln St
E Taylor St
E Gordon St
E Gordon La
E Gaston St
E Huntingdon St
Abercorn St

Whitefield Sq

11 ✕
Troup Sq

E Taylor St

E Gaston La
E Huntingdon St
Habersham St

E Broad St

Price St

12 ✕

For reviews see

⊙	Top Sights	p108
⊙	Sights	p114
✕	Eating	p116
✕	Drinking	p118
🛍	Shopping	p119

200 m
0.1 miles

Sights

Mercer-Williams House
HISTORIC BUILDING

1 ◎ MAP P112, C6

Although Jim Williams, the Savannah art dealer portrayed by Kevin Spacey in the film version of *Midnight in the Garden of Good and Evil,* died back in 1990, his infamous mansion didn't become a museum until 2004. You're not allowed to visit the upstairs, where Williams' family still lives, but the downstairs is an interior decorator's fantasy. (☏912-236-6352; www.mercerhouse.com; 429 Bull St; adult/student $12.50/8; ⏰10:30am-4:10pm Mon-Sat, noon-4pm Sun)

Telfair Academy
MUSEUM

2 ◎ MAP P112, C3

Considered Savannah's top art museum, the historic Telfair family mansion is filled with 19th-century American art and silver and a smattering of European pieces. The home itself is gorgeous and sunrise-hued – an artifact in its own right that wows visitors. (☏912-790-8800; www.telfair.org/visit/telfair; 121 Barnard St; adult/child $20/15; ⏰noon-5pm Sun & Mon, 10am-5pm Tue-Sat)

Sorrel Weed House
HOUSE

3 ◎ MAP P112, D5

Fans of the paranormal can get their thrills at one of Savannah's spookiest mansions – the ghost tours are genuinely creepy and the grounds hauntingly beautiful. (☏912-257-2223; www.sorrelweedhouse.com; 6 W Harris St; ⏰10am-11:30pm)

Flannery O'Connor Childhood Home
MUSEUM

4 ◎ MAP P112, E6

This stone row house on Lafayette Sq is where the literary great was born in 1925 and lived until she was 13. Her second short-story collection won the National Book Award in 1972 – eight years after she died. (☏912-233-6014; www.flanneryoconnorhome.org; 207 E Charlton St; adult/student $6/5; ⏰1-4pm Fri-Wed, closed Thu)

SCAD Museum of Art
MUSEUM

5 ◎ MAP P112, A3

Architecturally striking, this brick, steel, concrete and glass longhouse delivers your contemporary-art fix. There are groovy, creative sitting areas inside and out, and a number of rotating and visiting exhibitions that showcase some of the most impressive talents within the contemporary-art world. (www.scadmoa.org; 601 Turner Blvd; adult/child under 14yr $10/free; ⏰10am-5pm Tue, Wed, Fri & Sat, to 8pm Thu, noon-5pm Sun)

Jepson Center for the Arts
GALLERY

6 ◎ MAP P112, C3

Designed by the great Moshe Safdie, and looking pretty darn space-age by Savannah's standards, the JCA focuses on 20th- and

21st-century art. Be on the lookout for wandering scads of SCAD students (ha!) and temporary exhibitions covering topics from race to art in virtual-reality video games. (JCA; ☎912-790-8800; www.telfair.org/visit/jepson; 207 W York St; adult/child $20/15; ⏱noon-5pm Sun & Mon, 10am-5pm Tue-Sat; ♿)

American Prohibition Museum   MUSEUM

7 ◉ MAP P112, C2

Learn about the history of prohibition in the US in this spirited museum, the only one of its kind in the country. Exhibits feature live actors, films, animated portraits and detailed wax figures, and you can round out your visit with a tipple on the top floor at Up, the museum's speakeasy. (☎912-220-1249; www.americanprohibition museum.com; 209 W St Julian St; adult/child $13/10; ⏱10am-5pm)

Cathedral of St John the Baptist   CHURCH

8 ◉ MAP P112, E5

Completed in 1896 but destroyed by fire two years later, this impressive cathedral, reopened in 1912, features stunning stained-glass transept windows from Austria depicting Christ's ascension into heaven, as well as ornate Station of the Cross woodcarvings from Bavaria. (☎912-233-4709; www.savannahcathedral.org; 222 E Harris St; ⏱Mass 7:30am & noon Mon-Fri, noon & 5:30pm Sat, 8am, 10am & 11:30am Sun, in Latin 1pm Sun)

Sorrel Weed House

NATALIA BRATSLAVSKY/SHUTTERSTOCK ©

Historic District Tours

Learn about the side of Savannah that didn't make it into the history books with Vaughnette Goode-Walker's **Footprints of Savannah** (Map p112, D3; ☑912-695-3872; www.footprintsof savannah.com; tours begin in Wright Sq; adult/child $20/7; ⏱daily tours 10am), a 1½-hour walking tour that highlights the city's rich and complex African American history. Or if you prefer to learn on wheels, **Savannah Bike Tours** (Map p112, F3; ☑912-704-4043; www. savannahbiketours.com; 41 Habersham St; tours $25; ⏱varies by season) offers two-hour cycling excursions over easy flat terrain on its fleet of cruisers.

Eating

Husk Savannah   SOUTHERN US $$$

9 MAP P112, D3

After acclaimed success with Charleston, Nashville and Greenville locations, celebrity-chef Sean Brock brings Husk's hyper-local, agriculturally driven Southern food sorcery to Savannah. This outpost is the only one boasting a raw seafood bar and is the biggest of all, set in a historic, three-story space that hosts 200 people. Like all locations, the daily menu depends on what's locally available. (☑912-349-2600; www.husksavannah.com;

12 W Oglethorpe Ave; mains $25-36; ⏱5-10pm Sun-Thu, to 11pm Fri & Sat)

Treylor Park   SOUTHERN US $

10 MAP P112, E2

All the hip young things pack into this 'Treylor Park,' which revels in a retro-chic, Airstream aesthetic. The food? Southern classics simply done well: fried chicken on a biscuit with sausage gravy and spicy collard greens, or a grilled apple-pie sandwich. Take your pick and wash it down with an excellent cocktail in the warmly lit courtyard. (☑888-873-9567, 912-495-5557; www. treylorparksavannah.com; 115 E Bay St; mains $6-14; ⏱noon-midnight Mon-Wed, from 10am Sat & Sun)

Fox & Fig   VEGAN $

11 MAP P112, E6

A range of internationally inspired dishes get plant-based treatments at this charming cafe. Try the seared Southern seitan (wheat gluten) with French toast if you want a fix of something more indulgent but could do without the chicken-fried guilt. (☑912-297-6759; www.foxandfigcafe.com; 321 Habersham St; mains $7-16; ⏱8am-9pm Tue-Sun, to 3pm Mon)

Mrs Wilkes Dining Room   SOUTHERN US $$

12 MAP P112, C6

The line outside can begin as early as 8am at this first-come, first-served Southern comfort-food institution. Once the lunch bell rings and you are seated family-style, the kitchen unloads on you: fried chicken, beef stew, meatloaf, cheese potatoes, collard greens, black-eyed peas, mac 'n' cheese, rutabaga, candied yams, squash casserole, creamed corn *and* biscuits. It's like Thanksgiving and the Last Supper rolled into one massive feast, chased with sweet tea. (www.mrswilkes.com; 107 W Jones St; lunch adult/child $22/11; ⏱11am-2pm Mon-Fri Feb-Dec; 👫)

Little Duck   DINER $

13 🍴 MAP P112, D2

Classic diner fare gets reimagined in this bright, airy, art-deco-inspired space. We love its dedicated grilled-cheese menu, where you can scale up the traditional variety with Gruyère and Havarti, or go all out with indulgent ingredients such as duck or smoked salmon – plus a bowl of tomato soup, as you do. Tacos, bowls and breakfast are all top notch. (📞912-235-6773; www.littleduckdiner.com; 150 W Saint Julian St; mains $8-15; ⏱10am-3pm & 5-10pm Mon-Fri, 9am-10pm Sat & Sun)

Collins Quarter   CAFE $$

14 🍴 MAP P112, D4

This wildly popular newcomer is Australian-owned and turns Aussie-roasted Brooklyn coffee into beloved flat whites and long blacks. Beyond Savannah's best coffee, it serves excellent fusion fare, including a drool-inducing brisket burger. There's booze too! (📞912-777-4147; www.thecollinsquarter.com; 151 Bull St;

dinner mains $17-32; ⏱6:30am-5pm Mon, to noon Tue, to 10pm Wed-Sun; 📶)

Olde Pink House   SOUTHERN US $$$

15 🍴 MAP P112, E2

Classic Southern food done upscale in one of Savannah's most consistently great restaurants. Our favorite appetizer is the Southern sushi – shrimp and grits rolled in a coconut-crusted nori roll. Dine in the slender digs upstairs, or go underground to the fabulous tavern where the piano player rumbles and the room is cozy, funky and perfect. The building is a 1771 landmark. (📞912-232-4286; 23 Abercorn St; mains $15-43; ⏱11am-2:30pm, 5-10:30pm, closed lunch Sun & Mon)

Prohibition   AMERICAN $$$

16 🍴 MAP P112, B3

This sleek, dimly lit throwback restaurant and bar in a speakeasy style serves upmarket small plates, hearty entrées and bespoke cocktails for lunch, brunch and dinner. There's a stage for live bands, and a Sunday supper club is in the works. (📞912-200-9255; www.prohibitionsavannah.com; 125 Martin Luther King Jr Blvd; dinner mains $15-36; ⏱11am-2:30pm, 5pm-1am)

The Grey   MODERN AMERICAN $$$

17 🍴 MAP P112, B2

A wonderfully retro makeover of the 1960s Greyhound Bus Terminal gives us one of Savannah's culinary darlings, where

Famous Ice Cream

The classically American **Leopold's Ice Cream** (Map p112, F3; ☎912-234-4442; www.leopolds icecream.com; 212 E Broughton St; scoops $4-5.50; ☺11am-10pm Sun-Thu, to 11pm Fri & Sat; 🛜) has been scooping up its creamy Greek recipes since 1919. Tutti-frutti was invented here, but we dig the coconut, ginger, and honey and almond cream.

chef Mashama Bailey's 'Port City Southern' cuisine is a delightful, immigrant-infused take on local grub. Bearded hipsters work the best seats in the house, around the U-shaped centerpiece bar, where scrumptious lamb shoulder and a gargantuan pork shank are standouts. Reservations essential. (☎912-662-5999; www. thegreyrestaurant.com; 109 Martin Luther King Jr Blvd; mains $14-38; ☺5:30-10pm Sun & Tue-Thu, to 11pm Fri & Sat; 🛜)

Drinking

El-Rocko Lounge   COCKTAIL BAR

18 MAP P112, D3

One step in the door and you feel the '70s-inspired swank, but then realize the vibe – in true Savannah fashion – is absolutely chill. Friendly barkeeps mix fancy cocktails while DJs keep the energy high and dance moves steady with diverse jams on vinyl. The crowd is superhip but delightfully unpretentious, and the owner is as rad as they come. (☎912-495-5808; www.elrockolounge.com; 117 Whitaker St; ☺5pm-3am Mon-Sat)

Artillery   COCKTAIL BAR

19 MAP P112, D5

Talented mixologists craft novel, quality cocktails in this opulent space where elements of 19th-century eclecticism and romanticism meld with modern design touches. To drink here, abide by the house rules: no hats, sandals, tank tops, noisy phones, or shots. The signature Artillery Punch – a concoction of rye whiskey, gin, brandy and rum – packs a powerful punch. Sip slowly. (www. artillerybar.com; 307 Bull St; ☺4pm-midnight Mon-Sat)

Original Pinkie Masters   BAR

20 MAP P112, D5

Cheap, cash-only drinks and great people-watching make this hometown dive the best in town. It's far away enough from the River St ruckus, but easy enough to walk (err, stumble) to when you're ready to close out the night with the locals. (☎912-999-7106; www. theoriginalsavannah.com; 318 Drayton St; ☺3pm-3am Mon-Thu, noon-3am Fri & Sat)

Abe's on Lincoln   BAR

21 MAP P112, F3

Pop back a beer or 10 with SCAD students and locals at this dark, dank, all-wood bar. Abe's on Lincoln attracts an eclectic crowd that stares through boozy goggles at whatever weird behavior the bartenders are inevitably tolerating that night. Good times. (📞912-349-0525; www.abesonlincoln.com; 17 Lincoln St; ⏰4pm-3am Mon-Sat)

Rocks on the Roof

BAR

22 🚇 MAP P112, C1

The expansive rooftop bar at the Bohemian Hotel is breezy and fun. It's at its best when the weather is fine and the fire pit is glowing. (📞912-721-3821; www.bohemianhotelsavannah.com/dining/lounge; 102 W Bay St, Bohemian Hotel; ⏰11am-midnight Sun-Thu, to 1am Fri & Sat; 📶)

Distillery Ale House

BAR

23 🚇 MAP P112, B4

Formerly the Kentucky Distilling Co, which opened in 1904 and closed at Prohibition, this is oddly *not* Savannah's local throat-burning swill house, but rather its go-to craft-beer bar. It's also popular with tourists and families for bar food. (📞912-236-1772; www.distilleryalehouse.com; 416 W Liberty St; ⏰11am-11pm Sun-Wed, to midnight Thu-Sat)

Shopping

Books on Bay

BOOKS

24 🔒 MAP P112, D1

Junkies of that old-book smell will get a great fix at this quaint shop specializing in titles that date from the 17th century through

Olde Pink House (p117)

Understanding the Early History of Savannah

Georgia's history as one of the original 13 colonies began when James Oglethorpe and a group of inmate settlers sailed from England to Yamacraw Bluff on the banks of the Savannah River.

Early Land Disputes

In 1700 Spain, England and France all laid claim to the land that is now Georgia, deeming it 'the debatable land.' But it was the English who established the colony of Carolina in 1663 and began trading with tribes along the Savannah River. In 1712 the colony of Carolina was divided in two, North and South, and three years later the Yamassee tribe revolted against the English, resulting in the deaths of a large number of settlers. Though the revolt was abandoned and the Yamassee fled to Florida, it became apparent that some kind of 'buffer zone' between South Carolina and Florida was necessary.

There were several plans put forth, but all failed until James Oglethorpe came along. He was a young, visionary member of English Parliament who became concerned with the subhuman conditions of England's debtors' prisons after a friend of his died in one. To address the issue, he developed an idealistic plan: take the pressure off overcrowded debtors' prisons by bringing inmates to the New World to establish the buffer colony south of South Carolina. By 1732 Oglethorpe and a group of supporters convinced King George to approve the plan for the colony of Georgia to be settled on the banks south of the Savannah River.

The Establishment of Savannah

With an official charter issued, Oglethorpe and 114 colonists departed England aboard the *Anne* on November 16, 1732. After a three-month voyage, they arrived first in South Carolina where they negotiated permission to settle from Yamacraw tribe chief Tomochichi. The settlers then sailed through the mouth of the Savannah River and disembarked at Yamacraw Bluff on February 12, 1733. The city was founded on that date, and named Savannah.

Oglethorpe soon began work on plans for the city, along with co-planner William Bull. Loosely based on London as a model, it featured wards built around central squares in a grid. Trust lots for public buildings and churches were added on the east and west sides of the squares, and tithing lots for settlers' homes were laid out on the north and south sides; 22 of the original 24 squares still exist today.

the 1920s. Find 1st-edition runs of classics and works from literary greats, plus poetry collections, foreign manuscripts, religious and political texts and more. (📞912-236-7115; www.booksonbay.com; 224 W Bay St; 🕙10am-6pm)

ShopSCAD
ARTS & CRAFTS

25 🔒 MAP P112, D6

All the wares at this funky, kitschy boutique are designed by students, faculty and alumni of Savannah's prestigious college of art and design. There are a lot of awesome finds to be uncovered. (📞912-525-5180; www.shopscad.com; 340 Bull St; 🕙9am-5:30pm Mon-Fri, 10am-6pm Sat, noon-5pm Sun)

Civvies
VINTAGE

26 🔒 MAP P112, E3

Find some of the best vintage deals in town here – and once you've had a good run with your garments, they just may buy them back from you. The racks are well organized, the threads are solid quality and you'll find a handful of new, boutique-style selections as well. It's above a nondescript space full of antique furniture. (📞912-236-1551; www.civvieson broughton.com; 14 E Broughton St, upstairs; 🕙11am-7pm Mon-Sat, to 5pm Sun)

Satchel
FASHION & ACCESSORIES

27 🔒 MAP P112, D5

Handbag obsessives should definitely duck into Satchel, owned

and operated by the designer herself. She also manufactures her own goods and is a patron of all things design in Savannah. (📞912-233-1008; www.shopsatchel. com; 4 E Liberty St; 🕙10am-6pm Mon-Sat, 11am-3pm Sun)

Savannah Bee Company
FOOD

28 🔒 MAP P112, D3

This internationally renowned honey dreamland is one of Savannah's must-stops. Expect artisanal honey of infinite variety, and limitless free tastings. (📞912-233-7873; www.savannahbee.com; 104 W Broughton St; 🕙10am-7pm Mon-Sat, 11am-6pm Sun)

Explore

Midtown & the Victorian District

The residential architecture is astounding in this area, which was Savannah's first suburb and today is abuzz with a vibrant arts community and up-and-coming businesses. Admire the majestic homes from Forsyth Park to Victory Dr, the area's grand, palm-tree-lined avenue, and explore the galleries, museums, shops and restaurants that are shaping Savannah's local creative economy.

Bull St is the main artery running through this area, with Laurel Grove Cemetery being the sight furthest west, just on the edge of the Victorian District. Daffin Park is all the way east down Victory Dr, just before you approach East Savannah. Most sights, such as Star-land, right in the center, are easy to navigate by foot; beyond that, a car or bike is the way to roll.

Getting There & Around

The Victorian District is easily walkable, but if venturing to Midtown, bike, car or bus may be best. Bus lines 4, 11, 14, 27 and 28 all run from the **JMR Transit Center** (610 W Oglethorpe Ave) downtown to points further south, passing right through this area.

Midtown & the Victorian District Map on p126

Victorian District NORTHFORKLIGHT/GETTY IMAGES ©

Top Sight 📷
Laurel Grove Cemetery

While it may not have as much pop-culture hype and natural beauty surrounding it as Bonaventure does, Laurel Grove Cemetery is worth a visit for its spectacular monuments and rich history. Developed in 1850 as area cemeteries reached capacity, it served as the city's primary burial ground; the graves of many significant people throughout Savannah's history can be seen here.

◎ MAP P126, A4

2101 Kollock St

⊘ 8am–5pm

A Necropolis Divided

With two separate entrances, Laurel Grove is divided into two sections, north and south, by a highway. But more than a road divides them – Laurel Grove North was exclusively for whites, and Laurel Grove South for blacks.

The land that forms Laurel Grove today was once the Springfield Plantation, owned by one of Savannah's early colonists. Four acres of the original cemetery (the lowest, ill-drained point in a natural gorge, furthest from the city) was designated for the city's African American population, both free and enslaved. This was to replace the original graveyard in present-day Whitefield and Calhoun Sqs, which prevented southward expansion of the city. The acreage was then increased to 15, and doubled a few years later; the present allotment of 90 acres is roughly the same as Laurel Grove North.

Here Rests Savannah Society

Many notable Savannahians have been interred in both sections of Laurel Grove. On the north side, the most famed is Juliette Gordon Low, founder of the Girl Scouts of the USA, and more than 1500 Confederate soldiers are buried in a section devoted entirely to Civil War servicemen. In the south cemetery are graves of slaves and other African Americans who played an important role in the community's history, including Andrew Bryan, founder of the First African Baptist Church, and WW Law, a prominent leader in Savannah's Civil Rights movement.

All the plots in Laurel Grove North were sold off during the 1860s, but deceased Savannah residents continue to be buried in Laurel Grove South today.

★ Top Tips

● Ponder the gravity of the 'Stranger Burials' sign in Laurel Grove South.

● Try to visit either section of the cemetery first thing in the morning or last thing before they close – the light creates longer shadows for a more atmospheric effect.

● Look for the whipping tree at the center of Laurel Grove South, which still shows lash marks in its bark.

✕ Take a Break

Laurel Grove is within easy driving distance of the Historic and Victorian Districts. It's worth it to stop for a bite at one of the many cafes around Starland, such as Foxy Loxy (p129), in between visits to North and South.

Midtown & the Victorian District

HISTORIC DISTRICT

Forsyth Park

Sentient Bean

Drayton St

E Park Ave

Abercorn St

E Duffy St

E Henry St

E Anderson St

Bull St

W Duffy St

W Henry St

W Anderson St

W 31st St

Whitaker St

Howard St

W Gaston St

W Huntingdon St

Tattnall St

W Hall St

W Hall La

W Bolton St

VICTORIAN DISTRICT

W Park Ave

Barnard St

Jefferson St

Montgomery St

W Gwinnett St

Martin Luther King Jr Blvd

Habitat for Humanity

E Gwinnett Ct

Emerald St

May St

May St

W Anderson St

W 31st St

W 32nd St

Burroughs St

Floyd "Press Boy" Adams Park

Beecher Rd

W 34th St

Bock St

Lavinia St

Laurel Grove Cemetery

Laurel Grove Cemetery

500 m

0.2 miles

For reviews see

◎ Top Sights   p124
◉ Sights   p128
✖ Eating   p128
✖ Drinking   p129
⬤ Shopping   p131

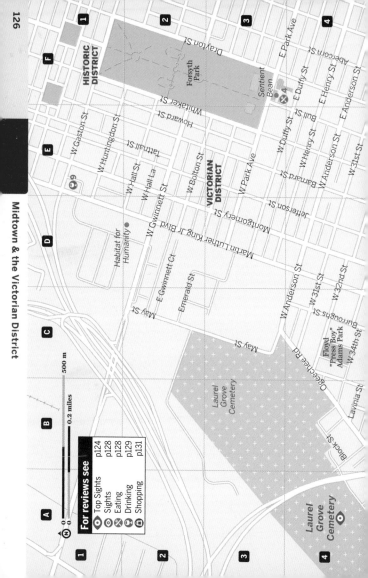

Midtown & the Victorian District

MIDTOWN

Thomas Square

Bull Street Library

Savannah African Art Museum 1

Old Savannah City Mission

Sulfur Studios

Chef Darin's Kitchen Table

E Victory Dr

West Victory Dr

West Victory Dr

E 31st St
E 32nd St
E 33rd St
E 34th St
E 35th St
E 36th St
E 37th St
E 38th St
E 39th St
E 40th St
E 41st St
E 44th St

W 32nd St
W 33rd St
W 34th St
W 35th St
W 36th St
W 37th St
W 38th St
W 39th St
W 40th St
W 41st St
W 42nd St
W 43rd St
W 44th La
W 44th St
W 45th St
W 46th St
W 47th St

W 34th St
W 35th St
W 36th St
W 37th St
W 38th St
W 39th St
W 40th St
W 41st St
W 42nd St

Habersham St
Lincoln St
Abercorn St
Drayton St
Bull St
Whitaker St
Barnard St
Jefferson St
Montgomery St
Martin Luther King Jr Blvd
Burroughs St
Florence St
Harden St
Bulloch St

Pratt Ave
Price St
Price St
Maupas Ave
Maupas Ave

Habersham St
Lincoln St

De Soto Ave
Howard St
Barnard St
Burroughs St
Florence St
Stevens St

Abercorn St

E 41st St
E 42nd St

Aline St
Kollock St
Ogeechee Rd

Stevens St
Bulloch St

Sights

Savannah African Art Museum

MUSEUM

1 MAP P126, E7

Privately owned museum showcasing 19th- and 20th-century spiritual and ceremonial art objects from 22 African countries, with museum volunteers giving guided tours. It was setting up its new premises at the time of research; check its Facebook page for an update on its reopening before visiting. (📞912-421-8168; visit.saam@gmail.com; 201 E 37th St; admission free; ⏰11am-4pm Thu-Sat)

Daffin Park

PARK

2 MAP P126, F8

This large recreational park has good walking paths, a pond, lots of grass for sports and picnics, and a public pool. You can catch baseball games at Grayson Stadium, home to the Savannah

Bananas baseball team. (📞912-351-3851; 1500 E Victory Dr)

Sulfur Studios

ART STUDIO

3 MAP P126, D7

Community art space with a gallery and retail space, plus open artist studios during Starland's First Friday Art March. (www.sulfur studios.org; 2301 Bull St; ⏰noon-5pm Thu-Sat)

Eating

Local11Ten

MODERN AMERICAN $$$

4 MAP P126, F3

Upscale, sustainable, local and fresh: these elements help create an elegant, well-run restaurant that's one of Savannah's best. Start with a blue-crab soufflé, then move on to the seared sea scallops in chive-lemon beurre blanc or the honey and brown-sugar rubbed pork chop and a salted-caramel pot de crème to finish. Wait. Scratch that. The menu already changed.

After dinner, head up to the rooftop bar for a digestif among the oak trees. (📞912-790-9000; www.local11ten.com; 1110 Bull St; mains $26-40; ⏰6-10pm; 🍸)

Green Truck

PUB FOOD $

5 MAP P126, F8

Casual pub serving locally sourced and housemade fare (right down to the ketchup). Its burgers are the best in town – we love the Trailer Park, adorned with pimento

---

First Friday ⓘ

On the first Friday of each month, galleries, shops and eateries around the Starland Arts District (which loosely radiates out from Bull St, just south of the Victorian District) open their doors for shows, shopping and drinking with local artists and makers.

cheese and bacon. (📞912-234-5885; www.greentruckpub.com; 2430 Habersham St; mains $9-14; ⏰11am-11pm Mon-Sat)

Narobia's Grits & Gravy
BREAKFAST $

6 ❌ MAP P126, F6

Lovers of soul food, seafood and breakfast food will get their fill with the simple, hearty plates at this humble hole in the wall. The French toast and crab biscuit aren't to be missed. (📞912-231-0563; 2019 Habersham St; ⏰7am-1pm Mon-Fri, to 2pm Sat)

Sweet Spice
JAMAICAN $

7 ❌ MAP P126, E8

This easygoing Jamaican spot, about 4.5 miles southeast of downtown, is a welcome break from all the American and Southern fare you get around here. A large platter of curry goat or jerk chicken costs just a smidge more than a fast-food meal and it's utterly delicious. It will also keep you filled up for a long time. (📞912-335-8146; www.sweetspicesavannah.net; 5515 Waters Ave; mains $6-14; ⏰11am-8pm Mon-Thu, to 9pm Fri & Sat)

Drinking

Foxy Loxy Cafe
CAFE

8 ☕ MAP P126, E6

Buzzing cafe and art-print gallery full of students and creatives set in an old Victorian house. The courtyard out back is the loveliest in this area. It has tasty tacos for

Laurel Grove Cemetery (p124)

when you get peckish, and freshly baked kolaches (fruit pastries) that are positively addictive. There's Sunday brunch, weekday happy hour, and monthly vinyl nights and poetry slams to boot. (📞912-401-0543; www.foxyloxycafe. com; 1919 Bull St; 🕑7am-11pm Mon-Sat, 8am-6pm Sun)

Chromatic Dragon

BAR

9 📍 MAP P126, E1

If the name of this place made you smile, you'll be right at home in this gamer's pub, which features video-game consoles, board games and drinks named for fantasy references, from *Harry Potter* butterbeer to fantasy role-playing game 'healing potions.'

There's a warm, welcoming atmosphere – truly, this is a certain kind of nerd's ultimate neighborhood bar. (📞912-289-0350; www. chromaticdragon.com; 514 Martin Luther King Jr Blvd; 🕑11am-11pm Sun-Thu, to 2am Fri & Sat)

Wormhole

BAR

10 📍 MAP P126, D7

This is a locally loved watering hole hosting live bands, comedy, DJs, trivia, open mics, karaoke and more.

There's pool, darts and video games to keep you plenty entertained while you catch a buzz, and it serves a full menu of food until late. (📞912-349-6770; www.worm holebar.com; 2307 Bull St; 🕑noon-3pm Mon-Sat)

Georgia peaches are prized across the nation; Georgia's nickname is the Peach State

Activities

Cooking Classes

When you tire of eating all that sinful Southern food (OK, that may never happen), try your hand at making it – along with dishes from other cuisines – with local top chef Darin Sehnert.

Theme-driven **cooking classes** (Map p126, E8; ☏912-662-6882; www.chefdarinskitchentable.com; 2514 Abercorn St, Suite 40; 4hr class from $75 per person; ⊙11am-6pm Tue-Fri, 10am-6pm Sat) include Low Country Cuisine, French Bistro and Northern Italian. There's also a store stocked with fine kitchen accoutrements.

Volunteering

Help Savannah's needy through **Habitat for Humanity** (Map p126, D2; ☏912-353-8122; www.habitatsavannah.com; 701 Martin Luther King Jr Blvd, ReStore; ⊙9am-5pm Tue-Sat), lending a hand with constructing homes for impoverished residents.

Or help **Old Savannah City Mission** (Map p126, D7; ☏ask for Connell Stiles 912-232-1979; www.oscm.org; 2414 Bull St; ⊙24hr) on a range of tasks.

Shopping

House of Strut
VINTAGE

11 MAP P126, D7

Our favorite vintage shop in town occupies the sprawling 1st floor of an old Victorian home, where each room is thoughtfully curated with unique, hand-picked fashion finds that are also available for rent.

The space doubles as a venue for local art and music events, and regularly hosts exhibitions, live performances and DJ dance parties. (☏912-712-3902; www.houseofstrut.com; 17 W 41st St, lower unit, ring bell to enter; ⊙11am-7pm Mon-Fri, 10am-6pm Sat, noon-4pm Sun)

Picker Joe's Antique Mall
ANTIQUES

12 MAP P126, E8

Pickin' and siftin' for antique and vintage treasures is a delight in this bright, clean, organized mall that was once a mattress factory. Military and aviation memorabilia is especially abundant due to owner Jim Plumlee's aviation background, and there's a room dedicated to architectural ornaments and fixtures. (☏912-239-4657; www.pickerjoes.com; 217a E 41st St; ⊙10am-6pm Mon-Sat, noon-5pm Sun)

Soul Food & the African American Diaspora

When it comes to perceptions of cuisine from this part of the country, the distinction between what's known as 'Southern' food and 'soul' food can be blurry.

While all soul food is Southern food, not all Southern food is soul – the roots of the latter stem from what was developed by African slaves in the Southeastern United States as they made do with whatever was available to them. As their descendants migrated north and west during the post-slavery era, they carried the traditional recipes of their forebears with them.

This diaspora brought about what is known today as soul food, a true American immigrant cuisine – in black communities outside the South, it's a celebration of down-home, rural roots, with traditional dishes being served usually only during special occasions. Typical ones include fried chicken and fish, ham hocks, oxtails, chitlins, pigs' feet, hush puppies and greens (collard, mustard or turnip). These parallel with a lot of Southern foods, though the soul variety is often fattier, saltier and spicier.

Traditionally, soul food wasn't as calorically offensive as we find it today. Its antebellum beginnings were based on seasonally available, organic (before the need for such a term was even a thing) produce, and meat was only used to add flavor to the vegetables. If meat was consumed, it was typically baked or boiled – frying was reserved only for celebratory occasions.

Processed ingredients such as refined flour, sugar and butter were only incorporated on the rare chance they could be obtained. In fact, with such a reliance on dark leafy greens, legumes, root vegetables and seafood, many of today's health fads and diet trends closely resemble early soul-food fare.

Savannah's Year in Food

While the eatin' is good year-round in Savannah, there are particular peaks for fresh produce and the local seafood industry.

May–August: Harvest time for beloved local produce such as Georgia peaches, field peas and okra.

Mid-June: Wild Georgia shrimp are at their biggest and most bountiful until the season comes to a close on December 31.

October–November: It's food and wine festival season, with events taking place almost every weekend.

Two Women & A Warehouse

ANTIQUES

13 🔒 MAP P126, D8

Interior designers and collectors will have a field day in this 7000-sq-ft warehouse, where more than 20 vendors peddle rescued and repurposed vintage and antique furnishings. (📞912-351-5040; www.2womenandawarehouse.com; 2819 Bull St; ⊙10am-6pm Mon-Sat, 1-5pm Sun)

Habersham Antiques Market

ANTIQUES

14 🔒 MAP P126, F8

There are plenty of great souvenirs to be found in Savannah, but we think you should snag an opulent chandelier or a Russian egg or some cool '70s cups or...

Coffeehouse Nightlife

The nightlife in midtown and the Victorian District has a distinctively local flavor, with lots of coffee houses doubling as after-hours hangouts. **Sentient Bean** (Map p126, F3; 📞912-232-4447; www.sentientbean.com; 13 E Park Ave; ⊙7am-9pm; 📶) is among the best of the bunch, with frequent live music.

look, whatever you want, really. Someone gave it up in the past, and it's now sold at this market. (📞912-238-5908; 2502 Habersham St; ⊙9:30am-5:30pm Mon-Fri, 10am-5pm Sat)

Explore ◈

East Savannah & the Islands

Welcome to a serene side of Savannah where expansive marshlands and winding estuaries slip into the sea. From the city's eastern edge and the riverside township of Thunderbolt, home to Bonaventure Cemetery (p136), past the residential enclaves of Whitemarsh and Talahi Islands, all the way out to the beaches of Tybee Island, great surf, seafood and scenery await by the Atlantic Ocean.

On the way to Tybee Island, you can admire the ramshackle homes along Bonaventure Rd before driving east on US Hwy 80, where you'll cross a tall bridge over the Wilmington River. From here, glowing grasses of the marshes fringe the road, which winds past portals to residential areas and a few shops, where you can grab any last-minute seaside provisions. Continue along Hwy 80 and pop into Fort Pulaski (p141) before crossing the final bridge to Tybee Island. There you'll find eclectic art shops and laid-back beach cafes along Butler Ave.

Getting There & Around

There's only one way on and off these islands. US Hwy 80 threads them all together, starting on the east side of town on Victory Dr, which eventually turns into Butler Ave on Tybee. The bus will only get you as far as Wilmington Island, so if you want to hit the beach, you'll have to go by car.

East Savannah & the Islands Map on p138

Tybee Pier (p141) AIMINTANG/GETTY IMAGES ©

Top Sight 📷
Bonaventure Cemetery

Nestled on the quiet banks of the Wilmington River, Bonaventure Cemetery is one of the world's most beautiful. Built on a former plantation, the mystical Southern Gothic tombs and monuments, set against a 100-acre natural landscape awash with ferns, azaleas, dwarf palmettos and Spanish-moss-riddled live oaks, conjure a serene reverence that's just the right kind of haunting.

◎ MAP P138, A2

📞912-651-6843, Historical Society 912-412-4687

www.bonaventure
historical.org

330 Bonaventure Rd

🕐8am-5pm

🅿

Famous Burials

Bonaventure was the final stop for many well-known Savannahians. Among the most famous grave sites is that of 'Little Gracie' Watson, a six-year-old local girl who died in 1889. Her father had a sculptor carve a detailed, life-sized statue of her from a photograph shortly before the grief-stricken family moved away from Savannah. To this day, visitors bring toys, flowers and other trinkets to her grave.

The cemetery is also home to the grave sites of Great American Songbook-era musician Johnny Mercer, whose family plot features a bench inscribed with lyrics from the singer's works; and Pulitzer Prize-winning poet Conrad Aiken.

Bonaventure in Pop Culture

Bonaventure's beauty became known to the world with the bestselling nonfiction novel and film *Midnight in the Garden of Good and Evil* (John Berendt; 1994). Characters in the book visit the cemetery and gossip over martinis at the grave site of poet Conrad Aiken, where a bench takes the place of a headstone. Scenes from the film, directed by Clint Eastwood, were also shot at the cemetery.

The famous *Midnight* cover features a statue of the *Bird Girl*, which sat virtually unnoticed until 1993 when Random House commissioned local photographer Jack Leigh for an image. After two days of searching for a subject, Leigh quickly captured the photo as dusk approached, then spent 10 hours in the darkroom developing it. The result was an eerie creation that appears awash in moonlight, and it became one of the most iconic photographs ever taken in Savannah. The statue became so popular from the success of the book that it was removed from Bonaventure and now sits on display in the Telfair Academy (p114).

★ Top Tips

o Book the Bonaventure After Hours tour with Bonaventure Cemetery Journeys (p140) for a chance to see the cemetery at night.

o Bonaventure Historical Society (www.bonaventurehistorical.org) offers free guided afternoon tours one weekend per month – check the website for dates.

o For self-guided tours, download the Bonaventure Historical Society's Bonaventure Cemetery Tour app.

✕ Take a Break

If you're in the mood for a picnic, Bonaventure has a handful of tables on the banks of the river. There are a couple of restaurants in Thunderbolt on River Dr, and in East Savannah off Skidaway Rd. Sisters of the New South (p142) is a great pick if you'd like a little soul food after communing with the dead.

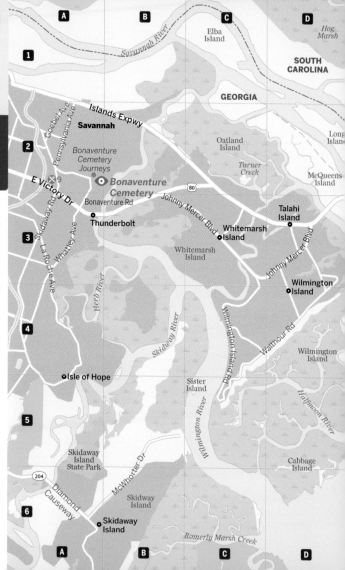

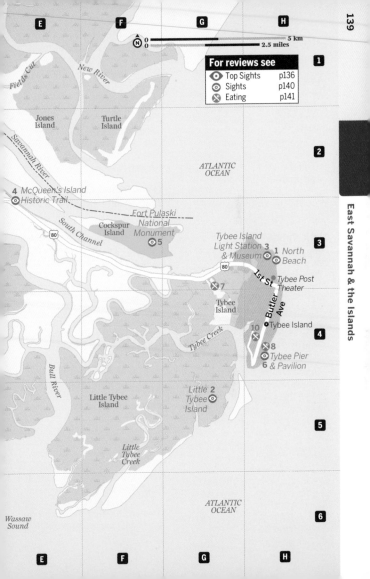

East Savannah & the Islands

For reviews see
- ◉ Top Sights p136
- ◉ Sights p140
- ✕ Eating p141

E

F

G

H

1

2

3

4

5

6

Fields Cut

New River

Jones Island

Turtle Island

ATLANTIC OCEAN

Savannah River

4 McQueen's Island ◉ Historic Trail

South Channel

80

Cockspur Island

Fort Pulaski National Monument ◉ **5**

Tybee Island Light Station & Museum ◉◉ **3 1** North Beach

80

1st St

Tybee Post Theater

✕ **7**

Tybee Island

Butler Ave

10 ✕ ◉ Tybee Island

Tybee Creek

✕ **8**
◉ Tybee Pier **6** & Pavilion

Bull River

Little Tybee Island

Little **2** Tybee ◉ Island

Little Tybee Creek

Wassaw Sound

ATLANTIC OCEAN

N 0   5 km
  0   2.5 miles

Sights

North Beach BEACH

1 MAP P138, H3

With fewer services and a vibe that feels more remote, this stretch of beach is a great place to relax. You can watch massive container ships drift in from sea, especially if you take a left once you hit the sand and walk further north up the shore to the point where the Savannah River runs into the Atlantic. (Railwood Ave, Tybee Island)

Little Tybee Island ISLAND

2 MAP P138, G5

This uninhabited barrier island, only accessible by boat or kayak, is just south of Tybee Island and

Cemetery Night Tour

Lovers of history will enjoy **Bonaventure Cemetery Journeys** (Map p138, A2; ☎912-319-5600; www.bonaafter hours.com; 330 Bonaventure Rd; $25-45 per person; ⊙day tours 10am & 2pm, night tour 5pm Sat) run by local historian Shannon Scott. The three-hour tour is the only way to see the cemetery at night, offering a different perspective on the history, architecture and traditions of Savannah's alluring city of the dead.

is actually double its size. The preserved land is rich with coastal marshland, dunes, wildlife and subtropical forests and is a great place to camp. There aren't any facilities on the island, but there's no fee and it's possible to visit any time.

Experienced kayakers can rent from any of the outfitters around Tybee, or book a charter service that runs trips to the island.

Tybee Island Light Station & Museum LIGHTHOUSE

3 MAP P138, H3

Take a self-guided tour of Tybee's iconic lighthouse and see panoramic views of the island from its observation deck. Tickets include admission to the nearby cottage and museum.

It accepts volunteers to greet visitors, interpret and help with on-site projects. Contact Gus Rehnstrom or Art Worden at 912-786-5801 or volunteers@ tybeelighthouse.org. (adult/child $9/7; ⊙9am-5:30pm Wed-Mon)

McQueen's Island Historic Trail WALKING

4 MAP P138, E2

This 6-mile walking and biking trail is built over a stretch of the Savannah & Atlantic Railroad line. It parallels the south channel of the Savannah River and you can spot wildlife such as box turtles, red-tailed hawks and brown pelicans.

The midpoint entrance is about 15 miles east of Savannah on US Hwy 80 on McQueen's Island, just as soon as you cross the Bull River; park along the road or at Fort Pulaski a little further along. (US Hwy 80, McQueen's Island)

Fort Pulaski National Monument   FORT

5 ⊙ MAP P138, F3

Located on Cockspur Island at the mouth of the Savannah River, Fort Pulaski was constructed after President James Madison ordered coastal fortifications following the War of 1812. For history buffs, it's worth a stop on the way to Tybee. (www.nps.gov/fopu/index.htm; adult/child under 16 $7/free; ⊙9am-5pm)

Tybee Pier & Pavilion   PIER

6 ⊙ MAP P138, H4

Tybee's main beachside hub, with public bathrooms, concessions and a long fishing pier. Tables in the pavilion are available to rent by the hour. (☏912-652-6780; 16th St at Strand Ave, Tybee Island; ⊙7am-11pm)

Eating

Crab Shack   SEAFOOD $$

7 ⊗ MAP P138, G3

This hidden favorite slings bountiful peel-and-eat seafood platters in a multishack complex along an alligator lagoon. Tables have a hole in the center with a giant Rubbermaid trashcan underneath, so you know it's legit

Fort Pulaski National Monument

(don't worry, the cats comin' for your scraps are kempt and dearly beloved members of the family). Get a spot on the patio, if you can. (🖉912-786-9857; www.thecrabshack. com; 40 Estill Hammock Rd, Tybee Island; mains $8-25; ⏰11:30am-9pm Sun-Thu, to 10pm Fri & Sat)

Breakfast Club

BREAKFAST $

8 🍴 MAP P138, H4

The line gets long (for a reason) but tables turn quickly at this family-owned breakfast favorite. Staples such as omelets are prepared with fresh ingredients, and they grind their own sausages and burger patties in house; the Blackhawk breakfast burrito is stellar. (🖉912-786-5984; www. thebreakfastclubtybee.com; 1500

Butler Ave, Tybee Island; mains $8-14; ⏰7am-1pm)

Sisters of the New South

SOUTHERN US $

9 🍴 MAP P138, A2

This laid-back cafe beloved of locals serves up Southern soul-food favorites for breakfast, lunch and dinner. The red-velvet cake is among the best we've tried. (🖉912-335-2761; www.thesistersof thenewsouth.com; 2605 Skidaway Rd; mains $6-14; ⏰6am-9pm Mon-Thu, to 10pm Fri & Sat, 8am-9pm Sun)

Tybee Island Social Club

AMERICAN $$

10 🍴 MAP P138, H4

Inventive starters, burgers, tacos and seafood dishes are best

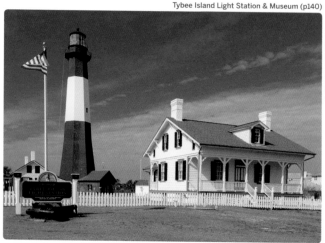

Tybee Island Light Station & Museum (p140)

638138O/GETTY IMAGES ©

Tybee Island

There are several shops on Tybee selling beach essentials – most are located along Butler Ave and on the side streets closer to the south end of the island. There are a few megastores on Whitemarsh and Wilmington Islands, but the options end there.

Nightlife on Tybee Island is limited to a handful of dive bars near the pier, and the occasional performance at the **Tybee Post Theater** (Map p138, H3; ☎912-472-4790; www.tybeeposttheater.org; 10 Van Horne Ave; ☉hours vary by event, check schedule). For a rollicking night out, trek back into town.

washed down with a signature cocktail at this laid-back haunt. The decor is modern with a touch of rustic, and a bluegrass band plays during brunch. It's a good spot to camp out and enjoy a bottle of wine (if you can nab a parking spot in the tiny front lot). (☎912-472-4044; www.tybeeisland socialclub.com; 1311 Butler Ave, Tybee Island; mains $9-18; ☉noon-10pm Mon-Thu, to midnight Fri & Sat, 11am-10pm Sun)

Worth a Trip 👀
Wormsloe Historic Site

Known for its iconic corridor of 400 live oak trees that stretch a mile from the entry gate to the main site, the colonial estate of Wormsloe was the first plantation established by the British in Savannah and, over the years, it has served as a military stronghold, a family country residence and a farm.

Getting There

Take Victory Dr east to Skidaway Rd for about 10 miles, then follow the signs; the grand entrance will be on the right.

Wormsloe's Establishment

Thanks to James Oglethorpe's friendship with Yamacraw tribe chief Tomochichi, the uninhabited land that would become Wormsloe was amicably acquired from the native tribe, and in 1737, four years after Savannah was established, the Isle of Hope peninsula was granted to three of the early colonizers. Noble Jones, a carpenter, was among them, and he obtained a lease of 500 acres that would eventually form the core of the site.

Strategic Defense

With establishment in Florida in the previous century, Spain retained loose control over the Georgia coast throughout the late 17th century (thanks to its Native American allies). This brought the Spanish into conflict with the English colonies in the Carolinas.

Their missions off the Georgia coast were subsequently destroyed, rendering the largely abandoned area a buffer zone between the Spanish and the English. When the English opted to colonize the land between Florida and South Carolina – prompting the arrival of Oglethorpe in 1733 – there was concern that the Spanish would attempt to oust them.

Sure enough, conflict broke out with the War of Jenkins' Ear. Wormsloe's strategic location on the Isle of Hope peninsula gave it a valuable role in defending the colony from Spanish attacks from the south. On his 500-acre plot, Jones constructed a fortified house of wood and tabby, a crude concrete composed of oyster shells and lime mortar.

The five-room, 1½-story house featured 8ft ceilings and bastions on all four corners, and was one of several protective outposts along Georgia's chain of barrier islands.

⊙ MAP P27

☏ 912-353-3023; www.gastateparks. org/wormsloe; 7601 Skidaway Rd; adult/ senior/child 6-17yr/ 1-5yr $10/9/4.50/2; ⊙ 9am-5pm daily; P

★ Top Tips

○ For a dramatic photo op of the Avenue of the Oaks in cooler, damper weather, visit first thing in the morning before the fog dissipates.

○ Follow the trail through the forest to the Moon River and see Battery Wymberly, military fortifications used during the Civil War.

○ Two guided tours are offered daily – call ahead to find out which topics will be covered on the day you plan to visit.

○ On anniversaries of historic dates or holiday weekends, check for special events with costumed demonstrations of colonial-era traditions.

✕ Take a Break

There are picnic tables on site – pack some food.

Survival Guide

Before You Go 148
Book Your Stay 148

Arriving in Charleston & Savannah 149

Getting Around 150
Bicycle 150
Boat 150
Bus 151
Car & Motorcycle 151
Taxi 151

Essential Information 151
Accessible Travel 151
Business Hours 152
Discount Cards 152
Electricity 152
Money 152
Public Holidays 152
Safe Travel 152
Toilets 153
Tourist Information 153

Rental bicycles in Charleston (p150) CSFOTOIMAGES/GETTY IMAGES ©

Before You Go

Book Your Stay

○ Savannah and Charleston both have a wealth of excellent sleeping options, although budget accommodations are tough to find.

○ Savannah experiences high-season tourism numbers from March to early June, but in the off season – particularly winter months (except for Christmas) – hotel rates can go down by triple digits.

○ Staying in the historic downtown is Charleston's most attractive option, but it's also the most expensive, especially on weekends and in high season.

○ The chain hotels on highways and near Charleston's airport offer significantly lower rates.

Useful Websites

Historic Inns & Boutique Hotels of Savannah (www.

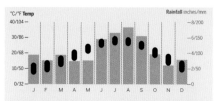

When to go

Spring and **fall** offer great weather and lots of festivals, drawing in lots of tourists willing to pay top dollar.

Summer is hot and muggy; locals and tourists head for the beach.

Winter is on the chilly side, but you can find good deals on lodgings.

bedandbreakfasts ofsavannah.com) Info and bookings for six premier Historic District properties.

Mermaid Cottages (www.mermaid cottages.com) Beach cottages and vacation rentals on Tybee.

Historic Charleston B&B (www.historic charlestonbedand breakfast.com) Connects visitors with small homes where owners serve Southern breakfasts and dole out local info.

Lonely Planet (www. lonelyplanet.com/ usa/the-south/ charleston/hotels) Recommendations and bookings.

Best Budget

Thunderbird Inn (www.thethunderbird inn.com) Roadside motel in Savannah with quirky, retro decor.

Not So Hostel (www. notsohostel.com) Charleston's only budget option is creaky, inviting and housed in a wonderful 1840 dwelling.

Savannah Pensione (www.savannah pensione.com) Bare-bones and basic accommodations in an old Victorian house.

Royal Palm Motel (www.royalpalmtybee. com) Budget motel with a tiny pool and an easy walk to Savannah's beachfront.

Best Midrange

Ansonborough Inn (www.ansonborough inn.com) An intimate Historic District hotel in Charleston with the vibe of an antique sailing ship.

Indigo Inn (www.indigoinn.com) Snazzy boutique inn right in the middle of Charleston's Historic District.

1837 Bed & Breakfast (www.1837bb.com) Charmingly over decorated inn near the College of Charleston.

East Bay Inn (www.eastbayinn.com) Traditionally furnished rooms in a historic Savannah inn.

River Street Inn (www.riverstreetinn.com) Waterfront inn housed in a former 19th-century cotton warehouse in Savannah.

Atlantis Inn (www.atlantisinntybee.com) Quaint rooms in Savannah with quirky murals and funky fixtures.

Best Top End

Kimpton Brice (www.bricehotel.com) Hip, ecofriendly boutique hotel in Savannah, with contemporary design elements.

Mansion on Forsyth Park (www.mansiononforsythpark.com) Opulent and sprawling Savannah mansion with views of Forsyth Park.

Beachview Bed & Breakfast (www.beachviewbbtybee.com) Laid-back, colorful and charming B&B a short walk from Savannah's beach.

Wentworth Mansion (www.wentworthmansion.com) A Gilded Age Charleston mansion loaded up with Tiffany stained-glass and hand-carved mahogany moldings.

Zero George Street (www.zerogeorge.com) Restored, circa-1804 stucco Charleston home with a fabulous restaurant.

Restoration (www.therestorationhotel.com) Boutique hipster enclave in Charleston, steeped in Americana arts-and-crafts kitsch.

Arriving in Charleston & Savannah

Charleston International Airport

Getting downtown from **Charleston International Airport** (Map p82, D1; ☎ 843-767-7009; www.chs-airport.com; 5500 International Blvd) is easy and fast with shuttles, taxis, buses, ridesharing and a rental-car center at your service. The airport is about 10 miles from the center of the city.

Savannah/ Hilton Head International Airport

From **Savannah/Hilton Head International Airport** (☎ 912-964-0514; www.savannahairport.com; 400 Airways Ave), rent a car, call a rideshare or catch a taxi to the Historic District for $28. Chatham Area Transit (CAT) operates the 100X Airport

Express route ($8 return) between the airport and the **JMR Intermodal Transit Center** (610 W Oglethorpe Ave) downtown.

Greyhound

Savannah's Greyhound Station (Map p112, A2; 📞 912-232-2135; www.greyhound.com; 610 W Oglethorpe Ave) sits right on the edge of the Historic District, and you can walk to your accommodations from here or catch a rideshare or metered taxi.

Charleston's Greyhound Station (Map p82, E1; 📞 843-744-4247; www.greyhound.com; 3610 Dorchester Rd) is in North Charleston, and it's simple to take a rideshare downtown. There's also a CARTA bus stop (route 11) in front of the station.

Amtrak

Savannah's Amtrak Station (Map p112, A4; www.amtrak.com; 2611 Seaboard Coastline Dr) is a few miles from the Historic District. Call a rideshare or metered taxi.

Charleston's Amtrak

Station (Map p82, E1; www.amtrak.com; 4565 Gaynor St) is in North Charleston, and taking a rideshare from here is simple. The adjacent CARTA stop (route 10) will also get you to the downtown area.

Getting Around

Bicycle

CAT Bike (www.catbike.bcycle.com; ⏱ daily/weekly membership $5/20, per 30min $2) is a bike-hire scheme run by Savannah's Chatham Area Transit. You have to buy a membership, after which it's free for the first hour. There are stations around town.

Charleston's flat terrain is ideal for bicycling. There are plenty of racks around town, and activists have been successful in getting some bike lanes and trails added. **Holy Spokes** (Map p64, D4; 📞 843-270-5346; https://charlestonbikeshare.com; 7 Radcliffe St, Suite 200; per hour/day $8/12; ⏱ 24hr)

is the city bike-share plan, with 27 locations downtown. A great rental place for longer periods is **Affordabike** (Map p64, D4; 📞 843-789-3281; http://affordabike.com; 573 King St; per day/week $25/55; ⏱ 10am-6pm Mon-Sat, noon-5pm Sun).

Boat

Charleston Water Taxi (📞 843-330-2989; www.charlestonwatertaxi.com; 10 Wharfside St; day pass adult/child $12/10; ⏱ 9am-8pm mid-Mar–mid-Nov, 10am-6pm Sat rest of the year) offers ferry service around Charleston Harbor, with stops at the aquarium, Patriot's Point in Mt Pleasant, the Charleston Harbor Marina and Waterfront Park. You can buy tickets online or on the boat.

There's also an Uber-style app for boats, called **HOBA** (www.hobarides.com). We're told it's a great way to get out on the water.

The free **Savannah Belles Ferry** (www.catchacat.org), designed in an old riverboat ferry style, connects downtown with Hutchinson

Island across the Savannah River. It has the following stops:

○ River St at City Hall

○ Waving Girl Landing at the Savannah Marriott Riverfront Hotel

○ Hutchinson Island at the Savannah International Trade & Convention Center

Bus

CARTA (☏ 843-724-7420; www.ridecarta.com) runs city-wide buses around Charleston; the one-way cash fare is $2. **DASH Trolley** (☏ 843-202-4410; www.charlestoncvb.com/blog/know-dash; ☉ schedules vary) has free streetcars that do three loop routes from the visitor center.

Savannah's **Chatham Area Transit** (www.catchacat.org) operates local buses that run on bio-diesel, including a free shuttle (the dot) that makes its way around the Historic District and stops near most major sights.

Car & Motorcycle

Most major car-rental companies, such as

Avis (☏ 843-767-7030; www.avis.com; ☉ 6am-midnight), have offices at Charleston International Airport. Be warned: parking is an issue. City parking lots charge around $2 per hour, and many hotels charge upward of $20 a night for parking.

Beyond the Historic and Victorian Districts of Savannah, transportation by car is the easiest means of getting around. Motorcycles are also seen citywide.

Taxi

Ridesharing apps are typically cheaper and easier than calling or finding a taxi, and many locals get around this way.

Essential Information

Accessible Travel

These cities are generally pretty friendly to travelers with disabilities, as most businesses are in compliance with ADA regulations, and ramps and elevators are available at most multilevel sights. That said, the uneven sidewalks and

Tipping

Tipping is *not* optional; only withhold tips in cases of outrageously bad service.

Restaurant servers 18% to 20%, unless a gratuity is already charged on the bill (usually only for groups of six or more)

Bartenders 15% to 20% per round, minimum per drink $1 standard drinks, $2 specialty cocktail

Taxi drivers 10% to 15%, rounded up to the next dollar

Hotel porters $2 per bag, minimum per cart $5

Hotel maids $2 to $4 per night, left in envelope or under the card provided

alleyways aren't great for wheelchairs.

There's free parking for people with disabilities in government-run parking areas.

Download Lonely Planet's free Accessible Travel guides from http://lptravel.to/AccessibleTravel.

Business Hours

Opening hours vary throughout the year. We provide high-season opening hours; hours will generally decrease in the shoulder and low seasons.

Banks 9am-5pm Mon-Fri

Restaurants 9am-10pm

Cafes 7am-7pm

Bars and clubs 5pm-2am

Shops 10am-6pm

Discount Cards

In both Savannah and Charleston, numerous sightseeing tour companies offer a range of packages with access to top sights. Visit kiosks around the cities' historic districts for coupons to individual attractions.

Electricity

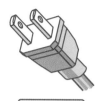

Type A
120V/60Hz

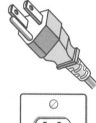

Type B
120V/60Hz

Money

ATMs are widespread, and credit cards are widely accepted.

Public Holidays

Major holidays and special events may mean many businesses are closed, or may attract crowds, making dining and accommodations reservations difficult.

New Year's Day January 1

Martin Luther King Jr Day Third Monday in January

Presidents' Day Third Monday in February

St Patrick's Day March 17

Easter March/April

Memorial Day Last Monday in May

Independence Day July 4

Labor Day First Monday in September

Halloween October 31

Thanksgiving Fourth Thursday in November

Christmas Day December 25

New Year's Eve December 31

Safe Travel

Charleston is a safe city with a relatively low crime rate, but dangerous and violent

Dos & Don'ts

Savannahians and Charlestonians ooze Southern charm and politeness. Don't be alarmed by people wanting to chat to you and learn your life story – and tell you theirs.

Greetings Handshakes are common when meeting men and women for the first time. Say 'hello' and 'goodbye' to staff when visiting shops, restaurants and sights.

Taboo topics It may be best to keep thoughts on US politics to yourself – you never know who you might offend. Also, Christian culture is overt; tread conscientiously with topics relating to religion.

Sensitivity about race These cities were centers of the slave trade, and places connected with that history should be treated with respect. For instance, when touring Charleston's Old Slave Mart Museum, it is not funny or OK to ask where you can get yourself a slave. (People have actually done this.)

crime is a reality in Savannah, with one of the highest rates in the US.

o Be vigilant and avoid walking alone at night in areas where there aren't a lot of people. That said, robberies have been known to happen in Savannah in broad daylight, even in parts of downtown with heavy tourist traffic.

o Don't leave valuables in vehicles in Savannah, as car break-ins and theft happen frequently.

Toilets

There are very few public restroom facilities in Savannah. Find them at Ellis Sq, the Bryan St and Liberty St parking garages, the Visitors Center on MLK Blvd and the River St Hospitality Center. The best public bathroom in Charleston is inside Charleston Place.

Tourist Information

Savannah Visitors Center (Map p112, B4; ☏ 912-944-0455; www.savannahvisit.com; 301 Martin Luther King Jr Blvd; ☉9am-5:30pm) Excellent resources and services are available in this center, based in a restored 1860s train station. Many privately operated city tours start here. There is also a small, interactive tourist-info kiosk in the visitor center at Forsyth Park.

Charleston Visitor Center (☏ 843-724-7174; www.charlestoncvb.com; 375 Meeting St; ☉8:30am-5:30pm Apr-Oct, to 5pm Nov-Mar) Find help with accommodations and tours or watch a half-hour video on Charleston history in this spacious renovated warehouse.

North Charleston Visitor Center (Map p82, E1; ☏ 843-853-8000; www.charlestoncvb.com; 4975b Centre Point Dr; ☉10am-5pm Mon-Sat, 1-5pm Sun) Has brochures, maps and staff who can help you plan your trip.

Survival Guide Essential Information

Index

See also separate subindexes for:

⊗ **Eating p156**

⊙ **Drinking p157**

✪ **Entertainment p157**

🔒 **Shopping p158**

A

accessible travel 151-2
accommodations 148-9
activities 20, 131
Aiken-Rhett House 46-7
airports 149-50
American Prohibition Museum 115
Anchorage 1770 100
Angel Oak Tree 84
art galleries 21, 128
ArtWalk 43

B

bathrooms 153
Battery 40
Beaufort 95-105, **96-7**
  food 100, 102-5
  sights 98-100
  transportation 95
Beauregard, Pierre 93
bicycling 150
Bill Murray Look-a-Like Polar Plunge 87
Bluffton 15
boat tours 20
boat travel 150-1

Sights 000
Map Pages 000

Bonaventure Cemetery 136-7
books 18
Boone Hall Plantation 57
Botany Bay Plantation Wildlife Management Area 85
Bulldog Tours 40
Bulls Island 86
bus travel 151
business hours 152

C

Calhoun Mansion 38
Cannonborough Elliotborough 61-75, **64-5**
  drinking 71-4
  entertainment 74
  food 67-71
  itineraries 62-3, **62**
  shopping 75
  sights 66
  walks 62-3, **62**
car travel 151
Cathedral of St John the Baptist 115-16
cell phones 24
Center for Birds of Prey 86
Charleston County Sea Islands 77-89, **82-3**

drinking 88-9
  entertainment 89
  food 86-8
  sights 78-81, 84-5
  transportation 77
Charleston Footprints 40
Charleston Museum 52
Charleston Tea Plantation 84
Chippewa Square 111
Citadel Campus & Museum 53
climate 148
Coastal Discovery Museum 99-100
College of Charleston 66
costs 24, 152
culture 58
currency 24
cycling 150

D

Daffin Park 128
dangers 152-3
Daufuskie Island 100
discount cards 152
Drayton Hall 57
drinking 12-13, see also Drinking subindex, individual neighborhoods
driving 151

E

East Savannah 135-43, **138-9**
  food 141-3
  sights 136-7, 140-1
  transportation 135
East Side 45-59, **50-1**
  drinking 56-5, 59
  entertainment 59
  food 53-6
  shopping 59
  sights 46-7, 52-3
  transport 45
economy 58
Edisto Island Serpentarium 85
Edmondston-Alston House 39
electricity 152
entertainment, see Entertainment subindex, individual neighborhoods
etiquette 153

F

ferry travel 150-1
Flannery O'Connor Childhood Home 114
Folly Beach County Park 84
food 10-11, 55, 71, 131,

132, *see also* Eating subindex, individual neighborhoods
Footprints of Savannah 116
Forsyth Park 108-9, 111
Fort Moultrie 84, 92-3
Fort Pulaski National Monument 141
Fort Sumter 91-2
Fort Sumter National Monument 90-3
French Quarter 31-43, **36-7**
  drinking 41-2
  entertainment 42-3
  food 40-1
  itineraries 34-5, **34**
  shopping 43
  sights 32-3, 38-40
  transport 31
  walks 34-5, **34**

G

Gateway Walk 68
gentrification 58
George Gallery 63, 66
ghosts 18
Gibbes Museum of Art 66
Gullah-N-Geechie Mahn Tours 101

H

Hampton Park 52-3
Hampton Park area 45-59, **50-1**
  drinking 56-7, 59
  entertainment 59
  itineraries 48-9, **48**
  shopping 59

sights 52-3
transport 45
walks 48-9, **48**
Harbour Town Lighthouse 99
Harleston Village 61-75, **64-5**
  drinking 71-4
  entertainment 74
  food 67-71
  itineraries 62-3, **62**
  shopping 75
  sights 66
  walks 62-3, **62**
hauntings 18
Henry C Chambers Waterfront Park 98
Heyward-Washington House 38
highlights 6-9
Hilton Head Island 95-105, **96-7**
  activities 102
  food 100, 102-5
  sights 98-100
  tours 102
  transportation 95
history 16-17, 18, 144-5
  Beaufort 104
  Charleston 43, 57
  Savannah 116, 120
holidays 152
Hunting Island 101
Hunting Island State Park 101

I

ice cream 118
Islands, the 135-43, **138-9**
  food 141-3
  sights 140-1
  transportation 135

itineraries 22-3, *see also individual neighborhoods*

J

Jepson Center for the Arts 114-15
joggling boards 41
Johnson Square 111
Joseph Manigault House 52

K

Kahal Kadosh Beth Elohim 73
Karpeles Manuscript Library Museum 63, 66
Kiawah Beachwater Park 84

L

language 24
Laurel Grove Cemetery 124-5
Little Tybee Island 140

M

Magnolia Plantation 57
Marion Square 66
McLeod Plantation 78-81
McQueen's Island Historic Trail 140-1
Mercer-Williams House 114
Middleton Place 57
Midtown (Savannah) 123-33, **126-7**
  drinking 129-30
  food 128-9
  shopping 131, 133
  sights 124-5, 128

transportation 123
mobile phones 24
money 24, 152
Monterey Square 111
motorcycle travel 151
Murray, Bill 87
music 13, 121

N

Nathaniel Russell House 38
NoMo 45-59, **50-1**
  drinking 56-7, 59
  entertainment 59
  food 53-6
  shopping 59
  sights 46-7, 52-3
  transport 45
North Morrison, see NoMo
North Beach 140
North Morrison, *see* NoMo

O

Old Exchange & Provost Dungeon 39-40
Old Slave Mart Museum 32-3
opening hours 152
Outside Hilton Head 102

P

Parris Island 101
Pat Conroy Literary Center 98
Pat Conroy Literary Festival 98
Pat Conroy's Beaufort Tour 102
planning 24
plantations 57
public holidays 152

R

Rainbow Row 40
Redux Contemporary Art Center 52
religion 73
restrooms 153
romance 19, 41

S

safety 152-3
Sandbar 98
Santa Elena History Center 98
Savannah African Art Museum 128
Savannah Bike Tours 116
Savannah's Historic District 107-21, **112-13**
  drinking 118-19
  food 116-18
  itineraries 110-11, **110**
  shopping 119, 121
  sights 108-9, 114-15
  transportation 107
  walks 110-11, **110**
SCAD Museum of Art 114
shopping 14-15, see also Shopping subindex, individual neighborhoods
Sorrel Weed House 114
South Carolina Aquarium 52
South of Broad 31-43, **36-7**
  drinking 41-2

entertainment 42-3
food 40-1
itineraries 34-5, **34**
shopping 43
sights 32-3, 38-40
transport 31
walks 34-5, **34**
spas 69
St Helena Island 101
St James Santee Parish Church 86
St Michael's Church 35
Sulfur Studios 128

T

taxis 151
telephone services 24
Telfair Academy 114
Telfair Square 111
time 24
tipping 24, 151
toilets 153
top sights 6-9
tourist information 153
tours 54, 116, 140
transportation 25, 149-51
Tybee Island 143
Tybee Island Light Station & Museum 140
Tybee Pier & Pavilion 141

U

Upper King 61-75, **64-5**
  drinking 71-4
  entertainment 74
  food 67-71
  itineraries 62-3, **62**
  shopping 75
  sights 66

walks 62-3, **62**
Urban Nirvana 69

V

Victorian District (Savannah) 123-33, **126-7**
  drinking 129-30
  food 128-9
  shopping 131, 133
  sights 124-5, 128
  transportation 123
Vintage Biplane Tours 102
visas 24
volunteering 131

W

walks
  Cannonborough Elliotborough 62-3, **62**
  Hampton Park 48-9, **48**
  Savannah's Squares 110-11, **110**
  South of Broad 34-5, **34**
water taxis 150-1
weather 148
websites 148
White Point Garden 40
Wormsloe Historic Site 144-5
Wright Square 111

⊗ Eating

167 Raw 53

B

Basic Kitchen 67
Bowens Island Restaurant 86

Breakfast Club 142
Brown Dog Deli 41

C

Callie's Hot Little Biscuit 47
Circa 1886 68
Cory's Grilled Cheese 88
Crab Shack 141-2
Cru Cafe 56

D

Darling Oyster Bar 68-9

E

Edmund's Oast 54

F

FIG 54-5
Fleet Landing 40
Fox & Fig 116

G

Gaulart & Maliclet 40
Green Truck 128-9
Grocery 71

H

Halls Chophouse 69
Harold's Cabin 55-6
Hominy Grill 70
Hudson's 102
Husk 70-1
Husk Savannah 116

J

Jack of Cups 87-8
Jasmine Porch 87
Java Burrito 100, 102
Juanita Greenberg's Nacho Royale 68

L

Le Farfalle 69
Leon's Oyster Shop 54
Leopold's Ice Cream 118
Lewis Barbecue 55
Leyla Fine Lebanese Cuisine 69-70
Little Duck 117
Little Jack's Tavern 55
Local11Ten 128
Lowcountry Produce 103-5

M

Marina Variety Store 70
Martha Lou's 55
Minero 41
Mrs Wilkes Dining Room 116-17

N

Narobia's Grits & Gravy 129

O

Obstinate Daughter 86-7
Old Bull Tavern 102-3
Olde Pink House 117
Ordinary 69

P

Plums 105
Poe's Tavern 88
Poogan's Porch 68
Prohibition 117

R

Red Fish 105
Ribaut Social Club 100
Rodney Scott's BBQ 55

S

Sgt White's 105
Shrimp Shack 101
Sisters of the New South 142
Skull Creek Dockside Restaurant 103
Slightly North of Broad 41
Sugar Bakeshop 63
Sweet Spice 129

T

The Grey 117-18
Treylor Park 116
Tu 54
TW Graham & Co 86
Tybee Island Social Club 142-3

W

Wild Olive 87
Workshop 58

X

Xiao Bao Biscuit 67

Z

Zero Café + Bar 56

🍷 Drinking

A

Abe's on Lincoln 118-19
Alley 74
Artillery 118

B

Bar at Husk 72-3
Bin 152 73-4
Blind Tiger 41

C

Carolina Cider Company & Superior Coffee 101
Charleston Distilling Co 72
Chico Feo 89
Chromatic Dragon 130
Closed for Business 72

D

Deep Water Vineyard 89
Distillery Ale House 119

E

Eclectic 71
Elliotborough Mini Bar 63
El-Rocko Lounge 118

F

Firefly Distillery 88
Foxy Loxy Cafe 129-30
Fuel 63

H

Hemingway's 105
High Wire Distilling 71-2

I

Ice Bing 74

K

Kudu 74

L

Low Tide Brewing 88-9

M

Moe's Crosstown Tavern 56

O

Original Pinkie Masters 118

P

Palmetto Brewing Company 57, 59
Pavilion Bar 42
Pour Taproom 72
Prohibition 72
Proof 72

R

Recovery Room 59
Revelry Brewery 56-7
Rocks on the Roof 119
Rooftop at the Vendue 42

S

Sentient Bean 133

W

Wormhole 130-1

🎭 Entertainment

Charleston Music Hall 74
Dock Street Theatre 42-3
Jazz Corner 105
Jinx 121
Joseph P Riley, Jr Park 59
Music Farm 74
Pour House 89
Savannah Smiles Dueling Pianos 121

Theatre 99 59
Tybee Post Theater 143
Windjammer 89

⊕ Shopping

B

Beads on Cannon 75
Blue Bicycle Books 75
Books on Bay 119, 121

C

Charleston City Market 43
Charleston Crafts

Cooperative 75
Civvies 121
Croghan's Jewel Box 75

E

Edmund's Oast Exchange 59

F

Farmers Market 75

G

Goat. Sheep. Cow. North. 59

H

Habersham Antiques

Market 133
House of Strut 131

I

Indigo & Cotton 75
Indigo Market 59

P

Picker Joe's Antique Mall 131
Robert Lange Studios 43

S

Satchel 121
Savannah Bee Company 121

Shops of Historic Charleston Foundation 43
ShopSCAD 121

T

Tavern at Rainbow Row 43
Two Women & A Warehouse 133

W

W Hampton Brand Gallery 43

Behind the Scenes

Send Us Your Feedback

We love to hear from travelers – your comments help make our books better. We read every word, and we guarantee that your feedback goes straight to the authors. Visit **lonelyplanet.com/contact** to submit your updates and suggestions.

Note: We may edit, reproduce and incorporate your comments in Lonely Planet products such as guidebooks, websites and digital products, so let us know if you don't want your comments reproduced or your name acknowledged. For a copy of our privacy policy visit lonelyplanet.com/privacy.

Acknowledgements

Cover photograph: Forsyth Park, Savannah, Richard Taylor/4Corners ©

Ashley's Thanks

Erin Morris for welcoming me to your state; Kourtnay King and Paul Haynes for taking me in and enabling me; Chandler Routman for getting me out of the house; Jason, Elizabeth, Iris and Loulou Ryan for being a great family; Patty Pascal for your unbridled enthusiasm; Halsey Perrin, Kim Jamieson and Ruta Fox for your help and expertize; and Chris Dorsel for still being amazing.

MaSovaida's Thanks

Thank you to the lovely souls in Savannah and beyond who provided tips, guidance and feedback. In particular, many thanks to Chad Faries and Emily Jones, Robert Firth and Trisha Ping for bringing me on. Special thanks and love to Ny, Ty and Haj.

This Book

This 1st edition of Lonely Planet's *Pocket Charleston & Savannah* guidebook was researched and written by Ashley Harrell and MaSovaida Morgan, and curated by Ashley. This guidebook was produced by the following:

Destination Editor
Trisha Ping

Senior Product Editors Vicky Smith, Kate Mathews

Product Editor Sam Wheeler

Senior Cartographer Alison Lyall

Book Designer Gwen Cotter

Assisting Editors Nigel Chin, Victoria Harrison, Alexander Knights, Kellie Langdon

Cover Researcher Naomi Parker

Thanks to Ronan Abayawickrema, Sandie Kestell, Angela Tinson, Amanda Williamson

Our Writers

Ashley Harrell

After a brief stint selling day spa coupons door to door in South Florida, Ashley decided she'd rather be a writer. She went to journalism grad school, convinced a newspaper to hire her, and started covering wildlife, crime and tourism, sometimes all in the same story. Fueling her zest for storytelling and the unknown, she traveled widely and moved often, from a tiny NYC apartment to a vast California ranch to a jungle cabin in Costa Rica, where she started writing for Lonely Planet. From there he travels became more exotic and farther flung, and she still laughs when paychecks arrive.

MaSovaida Morgan

MaSovaida is a Lonely Planet writer and multimedia storyteller whose wanderlust has taken her to more than 35 countries across six continents. Prior to freelancing, she was Lonely Planet's Destination Editor for South America for four years and worked as an editor for newspapers and NGOs in the Middle East and the United Kingdom. Follow her on Instagram @MaSovaida.

Published by Lonely Planet Global Limited
CRN 554153
1st edition – Dec 2018
ISBN 978 1 78701 441 1
© Lonely Planet 2018 Photographs © as indicated 2018
10 9 8 7 6 5 4 3
Printed in Singapore